TERRORISM GONE VIRAL: THE ATTACK IN GARLAND, TEXAS, AND BEYOND

HEARING

BEFORE THE

COMMITTEE ON HOMELAND SECURITY
HOUSE OF REPRESENTATIVES

ONE HUNDRED FOURTEENTH CONGRESS

FIRST SESSION

JUNE 3, 2015

Serial No. 114–19

Printed for the use of the Committee on Homeland Security

Available via the World Wide Web: http://www.gpo.gov/fdsys/

U.S. GOVERNMENT PUBLISHING OFFICE

95–683 PDF   WASHINGTON : 2015

For sale by the Superintendent of Documents, U.S. Government Publishing Office
Internet: bookstore.gpo.gov   Phone: toll free (866) 512–1800; DC area (202) 512–1800
Fax: (202) 512–2104   Mail: Stop IDCC, Washington, DC 20402–0001

COMMITTEE ON HOMELAND SECURITY

MICHAEL T. McCAUL, Texas, *Chairman*

LAMAR SMITH, Texas
PETER T. KING, New York
MIKE ROGERS, Alabama
CANDICE S. MILLER, Michigan, *Vice Chair*
JEFF DUNCAN, South Carolina
TOM MARINO, Pennsylvania
LOU BARLETTA, Pennsylvania
SCOTT PERRY, Pennsylvania
CURT CLAWSON, Florida
JOHN KATKO, New York
WILL HURD, Texas
EARL L. "BUDDY" CARTER, Georgia
MARK WALKER, North Carolina
BARRY LOUDERMILK, Georgia
MARTHA McSALLY, Arizona
JOHN RATCLIFFE, Texas
DANIEL M. DONOVAN, JR., New York

BENNIE G. THOMPSON, Mississippi
LORETTA SANCHEZ, California
SHEILA JACKSON LEE, Texas
JAMES R. LANGEVIN, Rhode Island
BRIAN HIGGINS, New York
CEDRIC L. RICHMOND, Louisiana
WILLIAM R. KEATING, Massachusetts
DONALD M. PAYNE, JR., New Jersey
FILEMON VELA, Texas
BONNIE WATSON COLEMAN, New Jersey
KATHLEEN M. RICE, New York
NORMA J. TORRES, California

BRENDAN P. SHIELDS, *Staff Director*
JOAN V. O'HARA, *General Counsel*
MICHAEL S. TWINCHEK, *Chief Clerk*
I. LANIER AVANT, *Minority Staff Director*

CONTENTS

TERRORISM GONE VIRAL: THE ATTACK IN GARLAND, TEXAS, AND BEYOND

Wednesday, June 3, 2015

U.S. HOUSE OF REPRESENTATIVES,
COMMITTEE ON HOMELAND SECURITY,
Washington, DC.

The committee met, pursuant to call, at 10:13 a.m., in Room 311, Cannon House Office Building, Hon. Michael T. McCaul [Chairman of the committee] presiding.

Present: Representatives McCaul, Smith, King, Duncan, Perry, Clawson, Katko, Hurd, Carter, Walker, Loudermilk, McSally, Ratcliffe, Donovan, Thompson, Langevin, Higgins, Richmond, Keating, Vela, Watson Coleman, Rice, and Torres.

Chairman MCCAUL. The Committee on Homeland Security will come to order.

The purpose of this hearing is to receive testimony regarding the increasing threat from violent Islamist extremist groups, such as ISIS, who use the internet and social media to recruit fighters, share propaganda, and inspire and potentially direct attacks.

Before I recognize myself for an opening statement, I would like to welcome our newest Member of the committee, Congressman Daniel Donovan of New York. We have another yet another New Yorker on this committee. Quite a contingency we are building. But his experience as a district attorney and dedication to public service make him a, I believe, valuable asset to this committee, and we are happy to have you, sir. I appreciate it.

I now recognize—I yield to the gentleman from New York.

Mr. KING. I would like to join you in welcoming Mr. Donovan. I have known him for many years. He is an outstanding district attorney, outstanding public servant, and he is going to be able to work across the aisle for the betterment of the country.

So, Dan, it is great to have you on board.

Chairman MCCAUL. Miss Rice is recognized.

Miss RICE. Just to show how bipartisan we are all going to be, as a Democrat, I would like to welcome my former colleague, D.A.—former D.A. Dan Donovan.

Great to have you here and look forward to working with you. Thank you, Mr. Chairman.

Chairman MCCAUL. Anybody else like to—Mr. Richmond?

Now on to a more serious topic, just yesterday in Boston reports are emerging that Mr. Rahim was killed by Federal law enforcement officers after lunging at them with a knife; he was being investigated by the Boston Joint Terrorism Task Force after commu-

(1)

nicating with and spreading ISIS propaganda on-line. Known associates of Mr. Rahim are also being arrested as we speak.

These cases are a reminder of the dangers posed by individuals radicalized through social media.

In Garland, 1 month ago, Elton Simpson fired off a series of tweets declaring his loyalty to the Islamic State and urged others to do the same. Simpson included a hashtag ''TexasAttack,'' previewing his decision to terrorize the Prophet Muhammad cartoon contest that Islamists on social media had singled out as a target.

In his final tweet, just minutes before the attack, Simpson told his followers to follow Junaid Hussain or also known as al-Britani, a 20-year-old British foreign fighter embedded with ISIS in Syria, and one of the group's top recruiters who has been linked to the CENTCOM Twitter hack in January of this year. Hussain was quick to praise the Garland attack and issued a warning that same night stating, ''The knives have been sharpened. Soon we will come to your streets with death and slaughter.''

This attack exemplifies a new era in which terrorism has gone viral. Extremists issued a call to arms to attack an event. A radicalized follower clearly heeded that call, and he took steps to make sure his act of violence would spread and motivate more.

Social media networks have become an extension of the Islamist terror battlefield overseas, turning home-grown extremists into sleeper operatives and attackers. The proliferation of jihadist propaganda on-line has established a new front in our battle against Islamist extremists. We are no longer hunting terrorists living in caves and who only communicate through couriers. We are facing an enemy whose messages and calls to violence are posted and promoted in real time over the internet.

For example, last month the threat level at military bases across the country was elevated after ISIS supporters posted the names of individuals serving in the military on-line and quickly spread this on social media. Aspiring fanatics can receive updates from hard-core extremists on the ground in Syria via Twitter, watch ISIS' bloodlust on YouTube, view jihadi selfies on Instagram, read religious justifications for murder on JustPasteIt, and find travel guides to the battlefield on ask.fm/Jihadi. Recruiters are mastering the ability to monitor and prey upon Western youth susceptible to the twisted message of Islamist terror.

They seek out curious users who question—have questions about Islam or want to know what life is like in the so-called Islamic State. They engage, establish bonds of trust, and assess the commitment of their potential recruits. From there, extremists direct users to continue the conversation on more secure apps where secured communications hide their messages from our intelligence agencies. Such communications can include advice for traveling to terror safe havens, contact information for smugglers into Turkey, or the membership process for joining ISIS itself.

I know the officials appearing before us here today are disturbed by these trends. Mobile apps, like Kik and WhatsApp, as well as data-destroying apps, like Wickr and SureSpot, are allowing extremists to communicate outside of the view of law enforcement.

Equally as worrisome are ISIS' attempts to use the dark or deep web. These websites hide IP addresses and cannot be reached by search engines, giving terrorists another covert means by which they can recruit fighters, share intelligence, raise funds, and potentially plot and direct attacks undetected, as we saw yesterday in Boston.

ISIS tailors its message for specific audiences around the globe and, in doing so, projects power far beyond its growing safe havens by amplifying its battlefield successes and winning over new converts across the world. Its media sophistication case helps legitimize its self-proclaimed caliphate and its perverse interpretation of Islam. This stands in stark contrast to al-Qaeda's past outreach, which relied on tightly-controlled, top-down messaging and propaganda more difficult for aspiring jihadists to find.

Today ISIS is instead taking a grassroots approach to terror, seeding its repressive world view from the ground up, from digital magazines to on-line videos that glorify barbaric murder. ISIS is using its multi-platform engagement to create a jihadi subculture that supports its violent ideology and encourages attacks against the United States and its allies.

These tactics are a sea change for spreading terror, and they require from us a paradigm shift in our counterterrorism intelligence and in our operations.

For example, we can start by doing what FBI Director Comey suggested, shaking the trees more aggressively to quickly identify and engage potential home-grown jihadis. But this is a dynamic new front in the war against Islamist terror. It will require a new approach with the heavy focus on the ideological battle space.

I am grateful for the three witnesses that we have here today that are dealing first-hand on the front lines with how this terror is going viral. I look forward to hearing their testimony and recommendations for confronting this new and dangerous challenge.

[The statement of Chairman McCaul follows:]

STATEMENT OF CHAIRMAN MICHAEL T. MCCAUL

JUNE 3, 2015

Just yesterday in Boston, reports are emerging that Usaama Rahim, who was killed by Federal law enforcement officers after lunging at them with a knife, was being investigated by the Boston Joint Terrorism Task Force after communicating with and spreading ISIS propaganda on-line. Known associates of Rahim are also being arrested. These cases are a reminder of the dangers posed by individuals radicalized through social media.

In Garland 1 month ago, Elton Simpson fired off a series of tweets declaring his loyalty to the Islamic State and urging others to do the same. Simpson included a hashtag ''TexasAttack''—previewing his decision to terrorize the Prophet Mohammad cartoon contest that Islamists on social media had singled out as a target. In his final tweet sent minutes before the attack, Simpson told his followers to follow Junaid Hussain, a 20-year old British foreign fighter embedded with ISIS in Syria and one of the group's top recruiters who has been linked to the CENTCOM Twitter hack in January of this year.

Hussain was quick to praise the Garland attack and issued a warning that same night: ''The knives have been sharpened; soon we will come to your streets with death and slaughter!'' This attack exemplifies a new era in which terrorism has gone viral.

Extremists issued a ''call to arms'' to attack an event, a radicalized follower clearly heeded that call, and he took steps to make sure his act of violence would spread and motivate more. Social media networks have become an extension of the Islamist terror battlefields overseas, turning home-grown extremists into sleeper operatives and attackers.

The proliferation of jihadist propaganda on-line has established a new front in our battle against Islamist extremists. We are no longer hunting terrorists living in caves who only communicate through couriers. We are facing an enemy whose messages and calls to violence are posted and promoted in real time.

For example, last month, the threat level at military bases across the country was elevated after ISIS supporters posted the names of individuals serving in the military on-line and quickly spread on social media.

Aspiring fanatics can receive updates from hard-core extremists on the ground in Syria via Twitter, watch ISIS bloodlust on YouTube, view jihadi selfies on Instagram, read religious justifications for murder on JustPasteIt, and find travel guides to the battlefield on Ask.fm. Jihadi recruiters are mastering the ability to monitor, and prey upon, Western youth susceptible to the twisted message of Islamist terror. They seek out curious users who have questions about Islam or want to know what life is like in the so-called Islamic State. They engage, establish bonds of trust, and assess the commitment of their potential recruits.

From there, extremists direct users to continue the conversation on more secure apps, where secure communication hides their messages from our intelligence agencies. Such communications can include advice for traveling to terror safe havens, contact information for smugglers in Turkey, or the membership process for joining ISIS itself.

I know the officials appearing before us today are disturbed by these trends. Mobile apps like Kik and WhatsApp—as well as data-destroying apps like Wickr and Surespot—are allowing extremists to communicate outside of the view of law enforcement. Equally as worrisome are ISIS attempts to use the "dark" or "deep web."

These websites hide IP addresses and cannot be reached by search engines, giving terrorists another covert means by which they can recruit fighters, share intelligence, raise funds, and potentially plot and direct attacks undetected.

ISIS tailors its message for specific audiences around the globe and, in doing so, projects power far beyond its growing safe havens by amplifying its battlefield successes and winning over new converts across the world. Its media sophistication helps legitimize its self-proclaimed Caliphate and its perverse interpretation of Islam.

This stands in stark contrast to al-Qaeda's past outreach, which relied on tightly-controlled, top-down messaging and propaganda more difficult for aspiring jihadists to find. Today, ISIS is instead taking a "grass-roots" approach to terror, seeding its repressive worldview from the ground up.

From digital magazines to on-line videos that glorify barbaric murder, ISIS is using its multi-platform engagement to create a jihadi subculture that supports its violent ideology and encourages attacks against the United States and its allies. Their tactics are a sea change for spreading terror, and they require from us a paradigm shift in our counterterrorism intelligence and operations.

For example, we can start by doing what FBI Director Comey suggested—"shaking [the] trees more aggressively"—to quickly identify and engage potential homegrown jihadis. But this is a dynamic new front in the war against Islamist terror, and it will require a new approach with a heavy focus on the ideological battle space.

I am grateful to have three witnesses today that are dealing first-hand with how terror is going viral. I look forward to hearing their testimony and recommendations for confronting this challenge.

Chairman MCCAUL. With that, I now recognize the Ranking Member.

Mr. THOMPSON. Thank you, Mr. Chairman. Thank you for holding today's hearing.

I would like to also thank the witnesses for appearing today.

On May 3, the American Freedom Defense Initiative, which is recognized as a hate group by the Southern Poverty Law Canter, organized a Muhammad art exhibit and contest event in Garland, Texas.

Two violent extremists armed with assault rifles and body armor attacked police that were providing security to the event, resulting in the wounding of a dedicated police officer. According to the FBI, just hours before the Garland attack, a bulletin was issued to State and local police stating that one of the assailants may have an interest in traveling to the event. Unfortunately, the local police stated that the bulletin was not received in time.

Mr. Chairman, by no means am I saying that this bulletin would have changed the outcome of the situation, but I do think that this illustrates that we need to continue looking into information sharing with State and local police and also listening to the boots on the ground on how to recognize and prevent acts of home-grown violent extremism.

In the days following the attack in Garland, supporters of the terrorist group ISIL praised the attack. After the attack, it was discovered that one of the gunmen detailed his plans to leave the country and travel to Syria to join ISIL on Twitter. The assailant's plans were disrupted when the FBI arrested some people that planned to travel with him. It also came to light that he engaged with other ISIL followers from around the world through Twitter.

Mr. Chairman, we know that the threats from foreign and domestic terrorist groups are not going away overnight. Using the internet and social media to recruit members, plan attacks, and spread ideology is not novel. As the director of the National Counterterrorism Center pointed out in a hearing in this committee in February, ISIL's exploitation of social media plays a prominent role in the group's ability to recruit fighters from around the world. But as we look at social media and how violent extremist propaganda is spread, we must look at ways to countermessage. Both sides of the aisle are engaged in an examination of the President's Countering Violent Extremism strategy. The Department has a vital role to play in carrying out that strategy, as evidenced by the fact that there is a dedicated CVE coordinator, David Gersten, working.

Mr. Chairman, at this time, I request that this committee have an open oversight hearing where we can take testimony from DHS's CVE coordinator about the Department's role in implementing the CVE strategy.

Furthermore, we know that more work remains to ensure that our foreign partners are willing to and able to stop and identify foreign fighters at their borders. Last Friday, the U.N. Council issued an unprecedented statement urging countries to enforce border controls that allow suspected terrorists to travel across international borders. The director of the NCTC also stated at our February hearing that there was work to be done in this area. I know that the committee has a task force that is examining this issue, and we should be receiving their recommendations soon.

Mr. Chairman, as I stated in our last hearing on this issue, we all have a stake to prevent terrorist attacks against Americans and on American soil. Accordingly, I encourage this committee to continue serious discussions on how to counter violent extremist messages while protecting Constitutional rights. As we consider this threat, we need to foster greater information sharing among diverse partners and seek new ways to work together to pursue effective and promising approaches to violent extremism.

With that, Mr. Chairman, I yield back.

[The statement of Ranking Member Thompson follows:]

STATEMENT OF RANKING MEMBER BENNIE G. THOMPSON

JUNE 3, 2015

On May 3, the American Freedom Defense Initiative, which is recognized as a hate group by the Southern Poverty Law Center, organized the "Muhammad Art Exhibit and Contest" event in Garland, Texas. Two violent extremists, armed with assault rifles and body armor, attacked police that were providing security to the event, resulting in the wounding of a dedicated police officer. According to the FBI, just hours before the Garland attack, a bulletin was issued to State and local police stating that one of the assailants may have had an interest in traveling to the event.

Unfortunately, the local police stated that the bulletin was not received in time. By no means am I saying that this bulletin would have changed the outcome of the situation, but I do think that this illustrates that we need to continue looking into information sharing with the State and local police and also listening to the boots on the ground on how to recognize and prevent acts of home-grown violent extremism.

In the days following the attack in Garland, supporters of the terrorist group ISIL praised the attack. After the attack, it was discovered that one of the gunmen detailed his plans to leave the country and travel to Syria to join ISIL on Twitter. The assailant's plans were disrupted when the FBI arrested some people that planned to travel with him. It also came to light that he engaged with other ISIL followers from around the world through Twitter.

We know that the threats from foreign and domestic terrorist groups are not going away overnight. Using the internet and social media to recruit members, plan attacks, and spread ideology is not novel. As the director of the National Counterterrorism Center pointed out in a hearing in this committee in February, ISIL's exploitation of social media plays "a prominent role" in the group's ability to recruit fighters from around the world.

But as we look at social media and how violent, extremist propaganda is spread, we must look at ways to counter-message. Both sides of the aisle are engaged in an examination of the President's Countering Violent Extremism strategy. The Department has a vital role to play in carrying out that strategy, as evidenced by the fact that there is a dedicated CVE coordinator, David Gersten.

At this time, I would request that this committee to have an open oversight hearing where we can take testimony from the DHS CVE coordinator about the Department's role in implementing the CVE strategy. We know that more work remains to ensure that our foreign partners are willing and able to stop and identify foreign fighters at their borders.

Last Friday, the U.N. Security Council issued an unprecedented statement urging countries to enforce border controls that allow suspected terrorists to travel across international borders. The director of the NCTC also stated at our February hearing that there was work to be done in this area. I know that the committee has a Task Force that is examining this issue, and we should be receiving their recommendations soon.

As I stated at our last hearing on this issue, we all have a stake prevent terrorist attacks against Americans and on American soil. I encourage this committee to continue serious discussions on how to counter violent extremist messages, while protecting Constitutional rights. As we consider this threat, we need to foster greater information sharing among diverse partners and seeks new ways to work together to pursue effective and promising approaches to counter violent extremism.

Chairman McCAUL. I thank the Ranking Member.

Let me first, I ask unanimous consent that the gentleman from Texas, Mr. Sessions, the Chairman of the Rules Committee, also represents Garland, Texas, be allowed to sit on the dais and participate in today's hearing.

Without objection, that is so ordered.

The gentleman from Texas is recognized, Mr. Smith.

Mr. SMITH. Mr. Chairman, I would like to ask unanimous consent to be recognized out of order for 2 minutes.

Chairman McCAUL. Without objection.

Mr. SMITH. Mr. Chairman, I appreciate your and the Ranking Member's indulgence.

I will yield my 2 minutes to the gentleman from Texas, the Chairman of the Rules Committee, Pete Sessions.

Chairman MCCAUL. Mr. Sessions is recognized.

Mr. SESSIONS. Mr. Chairman, thank you very much.

My thanks to Chairman Lamar Smith, my colleague from San Antonio, for kindly yielding time to me.

I also want to thank the young Chairman of the Homeland Security Committee, the gentleman from Austin, Michael McCaul, as well as the Ranking Member, my good friend, Bennie Thompson, and Members of the committee.

Thank you for inviting me to participate in today's hearing to discuss the ISIS-inspired terrorist attack in Garland, Texas.

As the proud Representative of the 32nd Congressional District of Texas, I am pleased to notify each and every one of you that all of north Texas is committed to fighting terrorism. Specifically, the city of Garland, Texas, is a diverse all-American city that continues to attract families and businesses with its thriving economy and growing opportunities. Since 1891, this city has grown from a small cotton-farming community to a thriving metropolitan area outside of Dallas with almost a quarter-million people that call Garland, Texas, home.

The mayor of Garland, Texas, Doug Athas is a friend of mine, and he works closely with his city managers, William Dollar and Bryan Bradford, as well as the police chief, Mitch Bates, and local officials, including the school board and other community leaders to ensure that Garland is a great, safe city to live in.

On Sunday, March 3—May 3, 2015, a courageous Garland police officer swiftly acted to protect the people of Garland from what could have been a devastating situation. I would like to commend the police officer and all members of local law enforcement who stood in the face of terrorism and protected countless innocent lives.

I remain committed to working with each of my colleagues in the House, local leaders, and local law enforcement to uphold our duty as elected officials to protect the people who we serve. It is my sincere hope at today's hearing, that we can learn positive lessons so that other cities and communities can be as prepared as Garland, Texas, if an event were to happen in their local community.

Mr. Chairman, thank you very much. I yield back my time.

Chairman MCCAUL. I thank the gentleman from Texas.

Other Members of the committee are reminded that opening statements may be submitted for the record.

Pleased to have a distinguished panel of witnesses before us today on this important topic. The first, John Mulligan, joined the National Counterterrorism Center in March 2015 as deputy director. Previously, he served as associate deputy director for counterterrorism at the National Security Agency.

Next we have Mr. Francis Taylor. Assumed his post as under secretary for intelligence and analysis at the Department of Homeland Security in April 2014. Previously, he served as assistant secretary of state for diplomatic security and director of the Office of Foreign Missions.

Finally, we have Mr. Michael Steinbach, who was appointed FBI director by James Comey as the assistant director of the Counterterrorism Division in July 2014. Prior to assuming his current position, he served as assistant director of the counterterrorism division and the acting section chief for the FBI's International Terrorism Operations Center.

I want to thank all of you for being here today.

The Chairman now recognizes Deputy Director Mulligan to testify.

STATEMENT OF JOHN J. MULLIGAN, DEPUTY DIRECTOR, NATIONAL COUNTERTERRORISM CENTER

Mr. MULLIGAN. Thank you, Chairman McCaul, Ranking Member Thompson, and Members of the committee. I greatly appreciate the opportunity to discuss some of the recent events of interest to the committee and the growing threat of extremists' use of social media to National security.

I am pleased to join my colleagues from Homeland Security and the Federal Bureau of Investigation. As you already know, we work closely every day as part of the counterterrorism community, and that interagency partnership is one of the keystones of our homeland defense.

This morning I will speak briefly to you about the recent attempted attack in Garland, Texas, and the role of violent extremist social media in that event. Then I will transition to broader remarks on ISIL's use of social media before concluding by sharing some of the efforts NCTC and our partners across the Federal Government are pursuing to counter that avenue of threat.

As has already been described, last month two U.S. citizens attacked an art exhibit and cartoon contest in Garland, Texas. The attackers arrived on the date of the event, exited their car, and opened fire with semiautomatic rifles, injuring a guard on the scene. Thankfully, local law enforcement partners in the area were aware of the potential for violence and were able to respond quickly to prevent the attack from injuring or killing others. This event highlights the growing threat our Nation faces from a new generation of terrorists, often operating from afar, who use social media to find like-minded associates within our borders who can be motivated to violence, attacking with little or no warning.

As was indicated, in this case, an on-line ISIL supporter on Twitter posted a link to an article with information about the cartoon contest a few weeks before-hand. This supporter's posting also included a message suggesting extremists should follow in the footsteps of the *Charlie Hebdo* attack in Paris.

Days later, one of the Garland attackers reached out to ISIL supporters and asked to move their communications to private Twitter messaging. The same individual also urged Twitter users to follow the account of a known ISIL member who had been trying to incite ISIL supporters to conduct attacks in the West. Just hours before the attack, the same attacker posted a message on his Twitter feed indicating he had pledged allegiance to ISIL with the accompanying hashtag "TexasAttack".

ISIL did not claim responsibility for directing or managing the attack, but ISIL operators praised the attackers and encouraged others to follow suit. The group also highlighted the attack in the most recent edition of its on-line magazine, which it publishes in several languages.

As we examine ISIL's broader efforts in social media, like any brand that seeks to target young people, ISIL continually innovates its on-line marketing to ensure it is developing effectively crafted messages. Using well-known U.S.-based platforms such as a YouTube, Facebook, or Twitter, ISIL works to ensure its media releases reach audiences far and wide through reposting, regeneration of follow-on links, and translations into multiple languages. ISIL also employs marketing tradecraft, attaching its messages to trending topics in order to gain additional readership. Consequently, its social media presence is more wide-spread than any other terrorist group.

Since the beginning of this year, ISIL has published more than 1,700 pieces of terrorist messaging. These include videos, pictorial reports, and on-line magazines. These products are often very professional in their presentation and timely in their delivery, underscoring ISIL's commitment to master multiple social media tools in order to advance their extremist objectives.

As the committee already knows, ISIL has often shaped its media contents to amplify the effect of its violent operations and activities. They do so in an attempt to project an image of power and intimidation. They also employ a complementary approach to enhance recruitment, a projection of the self-described caliphate as an idealized family-friendly environment in which ideological, religious, or personal fulfillment can be realized. This narrative has successfully induced large numbers of young people to make their way to the combat zones of Syria and Iraq.

During the past few months, ISIL's social media operators have more aggressively pursued a new line of effort. Following statements from senior ISIL leaders encouraging lone-actor attacks against the West, these operators are now practicing on-line recruitment and provisioning of terrorist instruction intended to precipitate civilian attacks within the United States and other nations. Sadly, as we have seen, some individuals have embraced the messaging and have sought to commit acts of violence on this basis.

When it comes to countering the spread of ISIL's violent messaging, several social media platforms have taken the initiative to close down accounts advocating terrorism and violent acts. They do this upon detection. However, energetic efforts to prohibit the propagation of violent messaging has not been universal, and there is still much work to be done to encourage greater vigilance and a broader sense of corporate responsibility to address this threat to public safety.

For our part, we are employing the knowledge that we have developed—that has been developed by the U.S. counterterrorism community to refine and expand our prevention efforts. We have seen a steady proliferation of more proactive and more engaged community awareness initiatives across the United States, all working with the goal of giving communities information and tools they need to identify the threats posed by violent extremist on-line recruitment and to effectively engage it before it manifests in violence.

With our DHS colleagues, we have created and regularly deliver a community resilience exercise program, a table-top exercise that brings together law enforcement and community leaders to run through a hypothetical scenario and potential responses.

In summary, we need multi-level partnership efforts to enable local U.S. communities to build the dual capabilities of addressing radicalization and ensuring resilient responses when an individual moves from radical ideology to radical violence. We must continue to develop our knowledge of evolving terrorist on-line tactics, and we need to communicate that knowledge so that it can be used to minimize the application of terrorist on-line tactics against our citizens.

I will stop there, Mr. Chairman. Thank you again for the opportunity to address the committee.

[The prepared statement of Mr. Mulligan follows:]

PREPARED STATEMENT OF JOHN J. MULLIGAN

JUNE 3, 2015

Thank you Chairman McCaul, Ranking Member Thompson, and Members of the committee. I appreciate this opportunity to discuss the potentially tragic event in Garland, Texas, last month, which we thankfully averted. And I want to more broadly address the growing threat of violent extremists' use of social media to our National security. I'm pleased to join my colleagues and close partners from the Department of Homeland Security and the Federal Bureau of Investigation.

GARLAND PLOT

As you already know, last month, two U.S. citizens attacked an art exhibit and cartoon contest in Garland, Texas. The attackers arrived on the last day of the event, exited their car, and opened fire with semi-automatic rifles, injuring a guard on the scene.

Thankfully, our law enforcement partners in the area were aware of the potential for violence and were able to respond quickly to prevent the attack from becoming a greater tragedy.

This event, however, exemplifies the challenge posed by home-grown violent extremists who can be motivated to violence quickly and have the means to attack without warning. It also highlights the growing threat our Nation faces from a new generation of terrorists who find like-minded associates on the internet and social media to share their violent extremist ideology.

GARLAND ATTACKERS' USE OF SOCIAL MEDIA

Let me explain more about how the Garland attack plans evolved. Less than 2 weeks before the attack, an on-line ISIL supporter posted a link on Twitter to a news article with information about the cartoon contest. This supporter's posting also included a message that suggested people should follow in the footsteps of the Charlie Hebdo attackers in Paris.

In addition, one of the Garland attackers reached out to the ISIL supporters and asked to move their communications to private Twitter messages.

Approximately 15 minutes before the attack, the same attacker posted a message on his Twitter feed indicating he had pledged allegiance to ISIL with the accompanying hashtag TexasAttack, which we now know was an indicator of his intent to target Garland.

While ISIL did not claim responsibility for the attack, many of its supporters, including a known ISIL member, praised the Garland attackers and encouraged others to follow suit. The group also highlighted the attack in its most recent edition of its English-language magazine *Dabiq*, in which it praised the attackers for seeking vengeance for the honor of the Prophet Muhammad.

BROADER COMMENTARY ON ISIL'S USE OF SOCIAL MEDIA

Like every other brand that targets young people, ISIL continually innovates to ensure it is using each new on-line marketing tool. Consequently, its social media presence—and that of its followers—is more wide-spread than that of any other terrorist group. In addition to maximizing its spread of terrorist messaging, the group shares guidance on how anyone can support ISIL and connects with like-minded individuals who become potential recruits.

In terms of the group's media efforts, ISIL has published more than 1,700 pieces of official terrorist messaging since the beginning of this year, including videos, pictorial reports, and magazines. These products are often very professional in appearance and continue to improve in quality with each new release, suggesting the group places a high priority on trying to win over the hearts and minds of new followers—including Westerners.

ISIL relies on the internet to send this material outside of Iraq and Syria and has shown a particular affinity for Twitter to disseminate official messaging, probably because the platform allows the group to reach a very broad audience. ISIL supporters also regularly use other platforms, such as Ask.FM and Facebook, to share information related to the self-declared Islamic State, including specific guidance on how to travel to Syria and how to avoid Western authorities.

ISIL supporters use the privacy of Twitter's direct messaging capability and encrypted messaging applications to discuss topics they deem too sensitive to display on their public accounts, such as travel facilitation into Syria or Iraq. We increasingly have seen ISIL supporters publicize their use of encrypted messaging applications on social media to let aspiring violent extremists and terrorists know that there are secure avenues by which they can communicate—after they make public contact on-line.

The group takes advantage of all the features and functions of social media to ensure wide-spread distribution of its messages. ISIL supporters on Twitter, for example, have used various tactics to expose its messaging to a more mainstream audience such as hijacking popular hashtags associated with pop culture figures or current events and using commercial applications to automate its tweets to make the group a trending topic.

It's important to be clear, however, that a video or series of pictures probably are not going to radicalize or mobilize to violence individuals who are just beginning to show interest in the group or violent extremist ideologies. Rather, these videos can serve as discussion points, which enable other ISIL supporters to find one another and discuss their support for the group with like-minded individuals.

During the past few months, numerous statements from senior ISIL leaders have called for lone-offender attacks against the West. We remain highly concerned by numerous people in the homeland who are buying into ISIL's distorted messaging. While we recognize companies have some initiatives underway to curb terrorist use of their platforms, there is still much work to be done.

COUNTERING VIOLENT EXTREMISM (CVE)

The volume of individuals going abroad as foreign terrorist fighters to Iraq and Syria only emphasizes the importance of prevention. Enduring security against terrorism—and defeat of terrorist organizations like ISIL—rests in significant part on our ability to diminish the appeal of terrorism and to dissuade individuals from joining them in the first place. To this end, we continue to refine and expand the preventive side of counterterrorism. Working in close coordination with the Department of Justice (DOJ), the Department of Homeland Security (DHS), and the Federal Bureau of Investigation (FBI), the National Counterterrorism Center (NCTC) is engaged in this work all across the country.

We collaborated with DHS to create tools that help build community resilience across the country. Additionally, we have seen a steady spread of proactive community awareness efforts across the United States. These efforts aim to give communities both the information and the tools they need to recognize violent extremist ideologies and to intervene before radicalization to violence.

In concert with DOJ, DHS, and FBI, NCTC met with communities in Denver, Sacramento, Buffalo, and Minneapolis to raise community and law enforcement awareness of the terrorist recruitment threat. Our joint presentation, developed in partnership with DHS, addresses the specific issue of foreign fighter recruitment in Syria and Iraq; and we have received a strong demand for more of this outreach.

This is an effort to share information about how members of our communities are being targeted and recruited to join terrorists overseas. This is not a law enforcement-oriented effort designed to collect information. Seen in that light, we have had a remarkably positive reaction from the communities with which we have engaged.

With our DHS colleagues, we have also created—and regularly orchestrate—the Community Resilience Exercise. This is a table-top exercise that assembles local law enforcement and community leadership in tackling a hypothetical violent extremist or foreign fighter-related scenario, including a hypothetical attack. The goal of the exercise is to build capacity within municipalities to mitigate the terrorist threat.

We are also encouraging our local partners to implement models for countering violent extremism similar to existing crime prevention efforts. This approach mirrors the way, for example, that local partners, including law enforcement, schools, social service providers, and communities, have come together to provide alternative pathways and outlets for people who might be vulnerable to joining a gang. We have found that the more resilient the community, the less likely its members are to join a terrorist group.

COUNTER-MESSAGING

As many community leaders have admirably pushed terrorist narratives out of their public spaces, these narratives have found refuge in virtual spaces. We understand that to truly counter violent extremist narratives, credible voices in communities should be encouraged to create alternative narratives that are attractive to target audiences. The role of these credible voices in communities as front-line responders cannot be overstated. Put plainly, we believe encouraging these community voices is an important and essential strategy.

However, communities best suited for repelling these terrorist narratives have not generally followed terrorist migration into on-line spaces. Communities whose young people are vulnerable to terrorist messaging have inconsistent capacities when it comes to countering that messaging. We believe this is the result of communities' fear of being associated with violent extremist elements, unfamiliarity with terrorists' on-line presence and tactics, and a lack of resources to create and disseminate alternative on-line content. Without confidence-building measures and proper training and resources, these communities will be hard pressed to counter ISIL's dominant messaging.

We are working with our partners and local communities to lessen these obstacles and to identify capacity-building measures. For example, we are connecting community leaders with entertainment industry executives. And we are actively trying to form public-private partnerships. For instance, the Peer2Peer program—a public-private partnership between EdVenture Partners and the Department of State—has empowered university students to create counter narratives to ISIL on social media. With programs like these, we have seen that private sector and community contributors can be much more nimble, creative, and credible on-line.

It is in everyone's interest to help mitigate this fear and encourage the use of law-abiding measures that communities can employ to confront terrorist narratives in virtual environments. To achieve this objective, we can provide training and information that will enable communities to use social and technical tools in the fight against on-line violent extremism. We can cultivate relationships between communities, the private sector, and the Federal Government based on trust and mutual benefit.

CONCLUSION

In summary, confronting these threats and working with resolve to prevent another terrorist attack remains the counterterrorism community's most important mission. This year, NCTC enters its second decade of service. While the Center has matured tremendously during that period, we are focused on positioning ourselves to be better prepared to address the terrorist threat in the decade to come. We expect this threat will increasingly involve terrorists' use of on-line platforms.

Chairman McCaul, Ranking Member Thompson, and Members of the committee, thank you for the opportunity to testify before you this morning. I want to assure you that our attention is concentrated on the security crises in Iraq and Syria—and rightly so. But we continue to detect, disrupt, and defeat threats from across the terrorist spectrum.

Thank you all very much, and I look forward to answering your questions.

Chairman McCAUL. Thank you, Mr. Mulligan.

The Chairman now recognizes Under Secretary Taylor to testify.

STATEMENT OF FRANCIS X. TAYLOR, UNDER SECRETARY, INTELLIGENCE AND ANALYSIS, U.S. DEPARTMENT OF HOMELAND SECURITY

Mr. TAYLOR. Mr. Chairman McCaul, Ranking Member Thompson, Members of the committee, thank you for the opportunity to appear with my colleagues to discuss the home-grown violent extremist threat to our country.

The terrorist threat today is more decentralized and complex. It is not constrained to one group, race, ethnicity, National origin, religion, or geographic location. ISIL, al-Qaeda, and other like-minded terrorist organizations have expanded their efforts to recruit individuals for violent action at home and to continue to be effective in recruiting foreign fighters from Western countries to travel to Syria and Iraq.

Core al-Qaeda and its affiliates remain a major concern for DHS. The group and its affiliates maintain the intent and in some cases the capability to facilitate and conduct attacks against U.S. citizens and facilities. Their attack planning continues, despite our persistent efforts to disrupt them.

Through their sophisticated messaging capability as Mr. Mulligan has mentioned, ISIL has been able to quickly reach a global audience and encourage acts of violence, inspiring U.S. citizens to travel to Syria to recruit and radicalize the violence—Western home-grown violent extremists here at home. This is concerning because mobilized lone offenders present law enforcement with limited opportunities for detection and to disrupt their plots. The recent attack in Garland, Texas, reinforced the importance of close collaboration and information sharing between DHS, the FBI, other Federal, State, local, and private-sector partners.

Prior to the attack, the FBI and DHS shared with the Texas fusion center and local law enforcement warnings that the event was at risk of being targeted for violent extremism. These warnings led to the preparations taken by the Garland PD that helped thwart the attack.

Our top priority to counter this evolving threat is information and intelligence sharing with our partners. DHS, I&A, and the National Protection and Programs Directorate's field personnel are instrumental in this effort and anticipate—to anticipate potential terrorist actions and to propose protective security measures that help build resilience in our communities across the country.

As an example of close coordination intelligence sharing between DHS, I&A, and our State and local partners was the protest last week in Phoenix, Arizona, this past weekend. We proactively contacted our partners on the ground and shared intelligence from the FBI and DHS sources in real time to help ensure local leadership and law enforcement had the necessary information to protect their communities and their citizens.

Additionally, we reached out to the faith community in Phoenix to provide information regarding the potential violent activities so that they could take preventative actions in their communities. It is important that we continue to build these partnerships with State and local law enforcement in a way that enhances community relationships and builds resilience to violent extremist recruitment.

DHS now has a senior executive, the DHS coordinator for countering violent extremism, whose sole role is to coordinate and improve the Department's CVE efforts. The new DHS CVE strategy emphasizes the strength of local communities and the premise that well-informed and well-equipped families, communities, and front-line personnel represent the best defense against violent extremism.

DHS will continue to work with our international counterparts and our colleagues within the FBI, NCTC, the State Department, and across the IC to identify potential threats to our security both at home and abroad.

Chairman McCaul, Ranking Member Thompson, and distinguished Members of the committee, thank you for the opportunity to appear before you today, and I look forward to your questions.

[The prepared statement of Mr. Taylor follows:]

PREPARED STATEMENT OF FRANCIS X. TAYLOR

JUNE 3, 2015

Chairman McCaul, Ranking Member Thompson, and distinguished Members of the committee, thank you for the opportunity to appear before you today—along with my colleagues from the Federal Bureau of Investigation (FBI) and the National Counterterrorism Center (NCTC)—to discuss the foreign fighter threat and current efforts to disrupt terrorist travel.

For some time, the U.S. Government, including the Department of Homeland Security (DHS), has been concerned that terrorist groups operating in permissive environments present a significant security threat to the United States and our allies. Events in Australia, Canada, and Europe underscore that the foreign fighter threat is no longer a problem restricted to foreign conflict zones such as those in Syria or Western Iraq. The Islamic State of Iraq and the Levant (ISIL) and other like-minded terrorist organizations have been effective in recruiting fighters from Western countries, as well as recruiting individuals for violent action at home.

The threat is real, continues to evolve, and is a present danger across the globe. The recent attack in Garland, Texas demonstrates the importance of close collaboration among I&A, FBI, NCTC, and our Federal, State, local, and private-sector partners. Prior to the art exhibit event at the Curtis Culwell Center, the intelligence community (IC) shared information with Texas fusion centers indicating the event had a risk of being targeted by violent extremists. When the perpetrators opened fire outside the exhibit on May 3, 2015, the attack was thwarted by the Garland Police Department. The information shared with Texas officials contributed to the overall threat picture and helped inform their security procedures for the event.

We recognize that the threat environment is ever-evolving and becoming increasingly complex and decentralized. For that reason, DHS is continuing to encourage an informed and aware public capable of self-advocacy, as promoted by the "If You See Something, Say Something™" campaign, as well as our more specific bulletins. We recognize protecting the homeland is a shared responsibility.

In my testimony today, I will discuss the foreign fighter threat and highlight specific efforts DHS is undertaking to identify, address, and minimize the foreign fighter threat to the United States and to our allies.

FOREIGN FIGHTER THREAT

While much of today's hearing will focus on terrorist threats from Syria and Iraq, it is important to emphasize that the terrorist threat is fluid and cannot be associated with one group, race, ethnicity, national origin, religion, or geographic location. Many terrorist groups continue to pose a risk to our security and safety.

Core al-Qaeda (AQ) and its affiliates, such as al-Qaeda in the Arabian Peninsula (AQAP), remain a major concern for DHS. Despite the deaths of many of AQ's senior leaders, the group and its affiliates maintain the intent, and, in some cases, the capability to facilitate and conduct attacks against U.S. citizens and facilities. The group and its affiliates have also demonstrated that capability to adjust tactics, techniques, and procedures for targeting the West.

Events in recent weeks have also made it clear why DHS and others in the counterterrorism and law enforcement communities are concerned about the threats posed by terrorists operating out of Syria and Iraq. In addition to al-Qaeda loyalists, a number of those involved in terrorist operations within Syria and Iraq are affiliated with ISIL. ISIL aspires to gain territory and attempt to overthrow governments in the region and eventually beyond. The group's experience and successes on the battlefields in Syria and Iraq have armed it with advanced capabilities that most terrorist groups do not have.

ISIL has also publicly threatened "direct confrontation" with the United States, which is consistent with the group's media releases since last summer that have alluded to attacking the United States. Through their sophisticated messaging capability, which includes the dissemination of high-quality media content on multiple on-line platforms, ISIL has been able to quickly reach a global audience and encourage acts of violence, as well as inspire U.S. citizens to travel to Syria to join in the conflict. Also on a daily basis, Syria-based ISIL members are attempting to recruit and radicalize to violence Western HVEs on social media, especially Twitter. The reach and popularity of social media has lowered the bar for Homegrown Violent Extremists (HVEs) to connect with terrorist organizations, such as ISIL.

ISIL's calls for lone offender attacks are likely resonating with HVEs because the group's self-proclaimed Caliphate resonates with individuals looking to be part of a larger cause, it regularly releases high-quality English-language videos and on-line magazines on-line, and their Western fighters are accessible on social media to HVEs interested in mobilizing. The IC assesses there is currently an elevated threat of HVE lone offender attacks by ISIL sympathizers, such as the Garland attackers, which is especially concerning because mobilized lone offenders present law enforcement with limited opportunities to detect and disrupt their plots.

The on-going conflict in Syria has emerged as a draw for more than 22,000 foreign fighters. More than 180 U.S. Persons and at least 3,700 Westerners have traveled or attempted to travel to Syria to participate in the conflict. We have also noted that veteran al-Qaeda fighters have traveled from Pakistan to Syria to take advantage of the permissive operating environment and easy access to foreign fighters. We remain concerned that foreign fighters from the United States or elsewhere who may go to Syria and Iraq, become more radicalized to violence, and return to the United States or their home country and conduct attacks on their own or in concert with others. Furthermore, we also are concerned that U.S. Persons who join violent extremist groups in Syria could gain combat skills and connections with violent extremists, and possibly become persuaded to conduct organized or lone-actor style attacks that target U.S. and Western interests abroad. We also are aware of the possibility that Syria could emerge as a base of operations for al-Qaeda's international agenda, which could include attacks against the homeland.

DHS RESPONSE TO THE FOREIGN FIGHTER THREAT

Aviation Security

Terrorist organizations like AQAP continue to pose a serious threat to international civil aviation. As we have seen in AQAP's three attempted aviation attacks against the homeland—the airliner plot of December 2009, an attempted attack against U.S.-bound cargo planes in October 2010, and an airliner plot in May 2012—terrorist groups have shown a significant and growing sophistication in terms of bomb design and construction, operational skill, and innovation. In the past 3 years terrorists have become increasingly interested in circumventing airport security screening through the use of improvised explosive devices (IEDs) concealed in cargo, commercial electronics, physical areas of one's body, in shoes or clothing, and in cosmetics and liquids.

To address the terrorist threat to aviation, DHS continues to evaluate, modify, and enhance aviation security measures. For example, beginning in July 2014, DHS required enhanced screening at select overseas airports with direct flights to the United States. Weeks later, DHS added additional airports to the list, with the United Kingdom and other countries following with similar enhancements to their required aviation security operations. Following recent world events, in January 2015, the Transportation Security Administration (TSA) took steps to enhance the number of random searches of passengers and carry-on luggage boarding aircraft at U.S. airports. TSA, as directed by Secretary Johnson, conducted an immediate, short-term review to determine if additional security measures are necessary at both domestic and overseas last-point-of-departure airports. DHS continues to evaluate the implementation of aviation security measures with air carriers and foreign airports to determine if more is necessary, and will make the appropriate aviation security adjustments without unduly burdening the traveling public.

In the long term, DHS is exploring the possibility of expanding pre-clearance operations at foreign airports with flights to the United States. This initiative provides for customs, immigration, and agriculture inspections of international air passengers and their goods by U.S. Customs and Border Protection (CBP) officials before the individual boards the plane for travel to the United States. Currently, CBP has pre-clearance operations at 15 airports and in 6 countries and, if appropriate, intends to enter into negotiations in order to expand air pre-clearance operations to new locations.

Information Sharing

Information sharing with our domestic and foreign partners is vital in identifying developing threats both here and abroad. DHS is committed to continuing our efforts, along with our colleagues in the IC, to partner with European governments and other key counterterrorism allies to share information about terrorist threats.

Since its inception, DHS has sought to broaden and deepen international liaison efforts to improve its ability to share information with key foreign allies. DHS has worked closely with the European Union through the U.S.-E.U. Passenger Name Records Agreement to facilitate the transfer of Passenger Name Records information to DHS by airlines that are subject to E.U. data protection laws. This agreement provides the highest standard of security and privacy protection. In addition, DHS has used its close partnerships with the countries in the Visa Waiver Program and the Five Country Conference to improve our respective abilities to identify illicit travel. The Preventing and Combating Serious Crime Agreement that DHS and 40 foreign partners have signed provides each signatory with reciprocal access to fingerprint repositories for the purposes of combating serious crime and terrorism. Along with the immigration authorities of Australia, Canada, New Zealand, and the United Kingdom, we participate in the Five Country Conference. We have been negotiating a series of bilateral immigration information-sharing agreements with those countries that would reduce the likelihood that a person applying for asylum or a visa in any of the five countries who has an illicit past could hide that history. DHS also engages with foreign partners to share analytic and targeting methodology, chiefly by conducting analytic exchanges, to enhance the ability of DHS and foreign allies to identify individuals and travel routes, and prevent foreign fighter travel to foreign conflict zones.

DHS is working with our interagency partners to inform our State, local, Tribal, territorial, and private-sector (SLTTP) partners of recent events and threats. Following the Paris *Charlie Hebdo* attacks, the Office of Intelligence and Analysis (I&A) prepared two Intelligence Notes and worked with the FBI to prepare and issue Joint Information Bulletins (JIBs); DHS shared both items Nation-wide with fusion centers. I&A field personnel, in partnership with DHS Office of Infrastructure Protection's Protective Security Advisors, are instrumental in threat information/intelligence dissemination to our SLTTP partners, characterizing threat information to jurisdictions, and proposing protective security considerations to prevent or mitigate terrorist activities. More recently, events in Garland, Texas highlight the critical importance of close collaboration between I&A and other Federal and SLTTP partners. The sharing of threat information concerning the art exhibit at the Curtis Culwell Center contributed to State and local law enforcement's overall threat picture for the event, which helped local authorities establish appropriate security procedures given the nature of the threat. Ultimately, the enhanced security posture helped prevent a potentially devastating mass casualty event.

I&A continues to provide our State and local law enforcement partners with information about observable behavioral indicators of U.S. Persons planning or attempting travel to Syria. I&A has produced tailored assessments on the motivations of U.S. travelers, their travel patterns, the role social media is playing in radicalization to violence, and the ways in which U.S. Persons are providing material support to Syria-based violent extremist groups. Additionally, I&A has partnered with the FBI to produce JIBs and other products for State and local law enforcement on the trends and observable behaviors in individuals seeking to travel to Syria.

Tracking Foreign Fighters

DHS is increasing efforts to track those who enter and leave Syria and may later seek to travel to the United States without a Department of State (DOS)-issued visa under the Visa Waiver Program (VWP). Working with the IC, DHS is working to ensure that individuals traveling from VWP countries are subject to enhanced vetting advance of travel to ensure National security and public safety.

In response, this fall, DHS strengthened the security of the VWP through enhancements to the Electronic System for Travel Authorization (ESTA). Through ESTA, CBP conducts enhanced vetting of VWP applicants in advance of travel to the United States in order to assess whether they are eligible to travel under the VWP or could pose a National security risk or public safety threat. Through interagency information-sharing agreements, CBP provides other U.S. Government agencies ESTA application data for law enforcement and administrative purposes to help assess risk and make a determination about an alien's eligibility to travel under the VWP without a visa. Additionally, CBP requires air carriers to verify that VWP travelers have a valid authorization before boarding an aircraft bound for the United States. ESTA has been a highly-effective security and vetting tool that has enabled DHS to deny travel under the VWP to thousands of prospective travelers who may pose a risk to the United States, prior to those individuals boarding a U.S.-bound aircraft. In response to increasing concerns regarding foreign fighters attempting to enter the United States through the VWP, DHS strengthened the security of the program through enhancements to ESTA. These improvements are designed to address the current foreign fighter threat, and provide an additional layer of security for the VWP. DHS determined that these ESTA enhancements would improve the Department's ability to screen prospective VWP travelers and more accurately and effectively identify those who pose a security risk to the United States. In addition, these enhancements to ESTA help the Department facilitate adjudication of ESTA applications. By requiring ESTA applicants to provide additional information, DHS can more precisely identify ESTA applicants who may be known or suspected terrorists. These enhancements also reduce the number of inconclusive matches that would previously have resulted in an ESTA denial.

Because we view advance passenger screening as a critical element to an effective National counterterrorism capability, we have explained to many partner nations how they can compare airline manifests and reservation data against terrorist watch lists and other intelligence about terrorist travel. This is an area where the United States has developed a capability significantly more advanced than most other nations, both in identifying illicit travel and in protecting the privacy and civil liberties of all travelers, and we have worked to share this know-how in order to prevent terrorists from traveling the globe in anonymity. Developing this capability is also consistent with the new obligations introduced through U.N. Security Council Resolution 2178, introduced last year by President Obama.

DHS is also working with partner nations in Europe, the Middle East, and North Africa to increase our information sharing to track Syrian foreign fighters. These efforts allow the United States greater visibility on potential threats to the homeland, while similarly enhancing our partners' ability to track and prevent terrorist travel. The importance of this issue was highlighted by the United Nations Security Council's adoption of Resolution 2178 in September 2014, which provided new momentum for European and other governments to use air passenger screening technology and enhance information sharing through multilateral and bilateral channels.

Countering Violent Extremism

HVEs from a range of ideological and religious backgrounds represent a persistent and often unpredictable threat based on their close familiarity with the United States and their ability to act with little or no warning as lone offenders or in small cells. Over the past few years we have seen HVEs plot to bomb high-profile targets, such as the Federal Reserve Bank in New York, the U.S. Capitol, and commercial establishments in downtown Chicago, Tampa, and Oakland. All these plots were disrupted.

To address the need to counter violent extremism (CVE) in the homeland and to guard against the domestic ''lone offender''—someone who did not train at a terrorist camp or join the ranks of a terrorist organization overseas, but is inspired here at home by a group's social media, literature, or violent extremist ideology—Secretary Johnson has directed DHS to build on our partnerships with State and local law enforcement in a way that enhances community relationships and builds resilience to violent extremist recruitment. DHS now has a senior executive, the DHS coordinator for countering violent extremism, whose sole responsibility is coordinating and improving the Department's CVE efforts.

To ensure a unified effort that fulfills opportunities and meets objectives, the Secretary recently tasked the DHS coordinator for countering violent extremism to update the current CVE Approach and develop a Department-wide CVE strategy. The new DHS CVE Strategy aims to improve the Department's ability to: Engage with local community partners; partner with the interagency and international community; provide best-in-class on-line innovation and analysis; and support CVE practitioners with research, training, and threat information. Under this strategy, DHS offices and components will prioritize CVE activities within their mission areas.

As part of the strategy, the Department plans to help cities and regions build and utilize local CVE frameworks for all forms of violent extremism threatening the homeland, and to encourage communities to develop their own intervention efforts to counter violent extremism. Within the limitations of appropriate Government action, we will address the evolving nature of on-line recruitment and radicalization to violence—particularly violent extremist use of social media—by encouraging credible voices to challenge and counter violent extremism.

Ultimately, this strategy aims to increase awareness among community members who may be in a better position to counter violent extremism. With increased training, analysis, and information sharing between the Department and State and local law enforcement, fusion centers, and first responders, we will increase the law enforcement understanding of violent extremism and how we can best mitigate threats.

DHS's approach emphasizes the strength of local communities and the premise that well-informed and well-equipped families, communities, and front-line personnel represent the best defense against violent extremism. Over the past 8 months, DHS has participated in a National Security Council (NSC)-coordinated interagency effort to work with Boston, Los Angeles, and Minneapolis/St. Paul to facilitate and support the development of locally-based, and -driven, violent extremism prevention and intervention pilot frameworks.

On February 18, 2015, the White House hosted a CVE Summit that focused on both domestic and international CVE efforts. Prior to the Summit, DHS hosted a roundtable discussion with Vice President Biden and domestic stakeholders on February 17, 2015, at the White House. The Summit included the rolling-out of piloted prevention and intervention programs in Boston, Los Angeles, and Minneapolis-St. Paul; DHS plans to evaluate these efforts and facilitate expansion to other municipalities. Under this initiative, DHS and the interagency encouraged local partners to develop mechanisms for engaging the resources and expertise available from a range of new partners, including the private sector as well as social service providers including education administrators, mental health professionals, and community leaders. As next steps, DHS is working with the interagency to further support prevention and intervention efforts in Boston, Los Angeles, Minneapolis-St. Paul and efforts elsewhere around the country while seeking to expand support efforts to other cities.

Additionally, since September 2014, Secretary Johnson has personally participated in direct engagement efforts with critical stakeholders in Chicago, Columbus, Minneapolis, Los Angeles, Boston, Boston and most recently, New York, to hear how DHS can best support local efforts to counter violent extremism and address foreign terrorist fighters. DHS CVE efforts, in partnership with NCTC, also include the development of the Community Awareness Briefing (CAB), which is designed to share Unclassified information with stakeholders regarding the threat of violent extremism, as well as help communities and law enforcement develop the necessary understanding of al-Qaeda, al-Shabaab, ISIL, and other entities' recruitment tactics as well as explore ways to address these threats at the local level. The CAB draws a parallel between the similar recruitment targets of all types of violent extremism. For example, the CAB uses the case study on the attack at a Sikh temple in Oak Creek, Wisconsin to illustrate potential for violence from all types of violent extremists, including but not limited to violent white supremacists, violent eco-terrorists, violent Neo-Nazis, criminal gangs (such as MS–13), and international terrorist groups. Due to the increased number of Western-based fighters traveling to foreign conflicts, such as Syria and Somalia, the CAB now includes information relating to the foreign terrorist fighter recruitment narrative by al-Shabaab and ISIL. CABs have been successfully conducted in 15 U.S. cities thus far.

Beyond our borders, DHS collaborates with partner countries, including the United Kingdom, Australia, Belgium, the Netherlands, Germany, Spain, and France, to develop best practices in community engagement endeavors that effectively counter violent extremism. Following the Paris attacks, DHS worked with some of these countries and DOS to link members of civil society and community stakeholders in respective countries so that they could coordinate and build grassroots responses to the attacks in Paris.

DHS is also working closely with the NSC staff, DOS, the Department of Justice including the FBI, and NCTC to prepare for the CVE Regional Ministerial Summit planned for June 11–12, 2015 in Australia. I will be leading the U.S. delegation to this summit, which will bring together key stakeholders from national and local governments around the world, as well as the private sector, civil society, and community leaders to develop an action agenda to address violent extremism in all its forms.

CONCLUSION

The terrorist threat is dynamic, as those who operate individually or as part of a terrorist organization will continue to challenge our security measures and our safety. DHS will continue to work with our international counterparts and our colleagues within the FBI and NCTC and across the IC to identify potential threats to our security, both at home and abroad.

Chairman McCaul, Ranking Member Thompson, and distinguished Members of the committee, thank you for the opportunity to appear before you today. I look forward to answering your questions.

Chairman McCAUL. Thank you Secretary Taylor.

The Chairman now recognizes Assistant Director Steinbach.

STATEMENT OF MICHAEL B. STEINBACH, ASSISTANT DIRECTOR, COUNTERTERRORISM DIVISION, FEDERAL BUREAU OF INVESTIGATION, U.S. DEPARTMENT OF JUSTICE

Mr. STEINBACH. Good morning, Chairman McCaul, Ranking Member Thompson, and Members of the committee. Thank you for the opportunity to appear before you today to discuss the reach of terrorist influence which transcends the geographic boundaries like never before.

Terrorists' use of technology has aided in the dissemination of rhetoric, encouraging attacks on U.S. interests in the homeland and abroad. As the threat to harm Western interests evolves, we must adapt and confront the challenges. This includes working closely with our Federal, State, local, and international partners since the threat persists in all of our communities. We continue to identify individuals who seek to join the ranks of foreign fighters traveling in support of ISIL and also those home-grown violent extremists who may aspire to attack the United States from within.

Conflicts in Syria and Iraq continue to entice Western-based extremists who wish to engage in violence. We estimate upwards of 200 Americans have traveled or attempted to travel to Syria to join extremist groups. We closely analyze and assess the influence groups like ISIL have on individuals located in the United States who are inspired to commit acts of violence. These threats remain among the highest priorities for the FBI and the intelligence community as a whole.

ISIL has proven relentless. Through their skillfully-crafted messaging, the group continues to attract like-minded extremists, including Westerners. Unlike other groups, ISIL has constructed a narrative that is appealing to individuals from many different walks of life. It is seen by many who click through the internet everyday, receive social media push notifications, and participate in social networks. In recent months, ISIL, via social media, has advocated for attacks against military personnel, law enforcement, and intelligence community members.

ISIL has gone so far as to post the names, addresses, and photos of U.S. military personnel to the internet, which quickly went viral.

We should also understand community and world events may entice an individual to act. As we have seen recently with highly-publicized events, including the attack in Garland, the events will attract media attention, and may inspire copycat attacks. The targeting of the Muhammad art exhibit and contest exemplifies the call-to-arms approach encouraged by ISIL, along with the power of viral messaging.

As I stated in previous opportunities I have had to testify before this committee, there is no set profile for the consumer of this propaganda. However, one trend continues to rise: The inspired youth. We have seen children and young adults drawing deeper into the ISIL narrative. These generations are often comfortable with virtual communication platforms, especially social media networks. Some of these conversations occur in publicly-accessed social media networking sites, but others take place via private messaging platforms. As a result, it is imperative the FBI and all law enforcement organizations understand the latest communication tools and are equipped to identify and prevent terror attacks in the homeland. We live in a technologically-driven society, and just as private industry has adapted to modern forms of communication, so too have the terrorists. Social media is yet the latest tool exploited by terrorists. With its wide-spread distribution model and encrypted communications, it has afforded a free zone by which to recruit, radicalize, plot, and plan. We need to urgently assess the laws applicable in these matters and work with private industry toward technology solutions.

To correct the narrative, this is not a conversation about National security at the expense of privacy or about weakening legitimate security of communication products through creation of technological back doors. We are looking to be fully transparent with the legal process showing evidence of a crime to gain access through the front door with full knowledge of those companies. The FBI seeks to ensure no one is above the law so the bad guys cannot walk away leaving victims in search of justice. There is certainly a balance between security and privacy. We seek that proper balance and one in which security enhances liberty.

The FBI, in partnership with DHS and NCTC, is utilizing all investigative techniques and methods to combat the threats these individuals pose to the United States.

In conjunction with our domestic and foreign partners, we are rigorously collecting and analyzing intelligence information as it pertains to the on-going threat posed by foreign terrorist organizations and home-grown violent extremists. In partnership with our many Federal, State, and local agencies assigned to Joint Terrorism Task Forces around the country, we remain vigilant to ensure the safety of the American public.

Chairman McCaul, Ranking Member Thompson, and committee Members, I thank you for the opportunity to testify concerning ISIL's persistent threat to the United States. I am happy to answer any questions you may have.

[The prepared statement of Mr. Steinbach follows:]

PREPARED STATEMENT OF MICHAEL B. STEINBACH

JUNE 3, 2015

Good morning Chairman McCaul, Ranking Member Thompson, and Members of the committee. Thank you for the opportunity to appear before you today to discuss the wide-spread reach of terrorists' influence, which transcends geographic boundaries like never before. As technology advances so, too, does terrorists' use of technology to communicate—both to inspire and recruit. The wide-spread use of technology propagates the persistent terrorist message to attack U.S. interests whether in the homeland or abroad. As the threat to harm Western interests evolves, we must adapt and confront the challenges, relying heavily on the strength of our Federal, State, local, and international partnerships.

We continue to identify individuals who seek to join the ranks of foreign fighters traveling in support of the Islamic State of Iraq and the Levant, commonly known as ISIL, and also home-grown violent extremists who may aspire to attack the United States from within. These threats remain among the highest priorities for the FBI and the intelligence community as a whole.

Conflicts in Syria and Iraq continue to serve as the most attractive overseas theaters for Western-based extremists who want to engage in violence. We estimate upwards of 200 Americans have traveled or attempted to travel to Syria to participate in the conflict. While this number is lower in comparison to many of our international partners, we closely analyze and assess the influence groups like ISIL have on individuals located in the United States who are inspired to commit acts of violence. Whether or not the individuals are affiliated with a foreign terrorist organization and are willing to travel abroad to fight or are inspired by the call to arms to act in their communities, they potentially pose a significant threat to the safety of the United States and U.S. persons.

ISIL has proven relentless in its violent campaign to rule and has aggressively promoted its hateful message, attracting like-minded extremists to include Westerners. To an even greater degree than al-Qaeda or other foreign terrorist organizations, ISIL has persistently used the internet to communicate. From a homeland perspective, it is ISIL's wide-spread reach through the internet and social media which is most concerning as ISIL has aggressively employed this technology for its nefarious strategy. ISIL blends traditional media platforms, glossy photos, in-depth articles, and social media campaigns that can go viral in a matter of seconds. No matter the format, the message of radicalization spreads faster than we imagined just a few years ago.

Unlike other groups, ISIL has constructed a narrative that touches on all facets of life—from career opportunities, to family life, to a sense of community. The message isn't tailored solely to those who are overtly expressing symptoms of radicalization. It is seen by many who click through the internet every day, receive social media push notifications, and participate in social networks. Ultimately, many of these individuals are seeking a sense of belonging.

As a communication medium, social media is a critical tool for terror groups to exploit. One recent example occurred last week. An individual was arrested for providing material support to ISIL by facilitating an associate's travel to Syria to join ISIL. The arrested individual had multiple connections, via a social media networking site, with other like-minded individuals.

As I've stated in previous opportunities I've had to testify before this committee, there is no set profile for the susceptible consumer of this propaganda. However, one trend continues to rise—the inspired youth. We've seen certain children and young adults drawing deeper into the ISIL narrative. These individuals are often comfortable with virtual communication platforms, specifically social media networks.

ISIL continues to disseminate their terrorist message to all social media users—regardless of age. Following other groups, ISIL has advocated for lone-wolf attacks. In recent months ISIL released a video, via social media, reiterating the group's encouragement of lone-offender attacks in Western countries, specifically advocating for attacks against soldiers and law enforcement, intelligence community members, and Government personnel. Several incidents have occurred in the United States and Europe over the last few months that indicate this ''call to arms'' has resonated among ISIL supporters and sympathizers.

In one case, a Kansas-based male was arrested in April after he systematically carried out steps to attack a U.S. military institution and a local police station. The individual, who was inspired by ISIL propaganda, expressed his support for ISIL on-line and took steps to carry out acts encouraged in the ISIL call to arms.

The targeting of U.S. military personnel is also evident with the release of hundreds of names of individuals serving in the U.S. military by ISIL supporters. The names were posted to the internet and quickly spread through social media, depicting ISIL's capability to produce viral messaging. Threats to U.S. military and coalition forces continue today.

Across the world, recent events commemorating ANZAC Day, a significant milestone in Australian and New Zealand military history, attracted unwanted attention that could have resulted in violence had Australian authorities not disrupted the plotting efforts underway. These arrests re-emphasize our need to remain vigilant in the homeland against these small-scale attacks.

We should also understand community and world events—as viewed through the eyes of a committed individual—may trigger action. As we've seen with recent highly-publicized events, including the attack in Garland, Texas, these acts of terror will attract international media attention and may inspire ''copy-cat'' attacks. The targeting of the Muhammad Art Exhibit and Contest exemplifies the call-to-arms approach encouraged by ISIL along with the power of viral messaging. In this instance, the event gained much publicity prior to it occurring and attracted negative attention that reached areas of the country—and the world—that it may not have without the wide-spread reach of the internet. The extensive network coupled with the magnetic messaging provides inspiration and validation that others share their outrage.

Lastly, social media has allowed groups, such as ISIL, to use the internet to spot and assess potential recruits. With the wide-spread horizontal distribution of social media, terrorists can identify vulnerable individuals of all ages in the United States—spot, assess, recruit, and radicalize—either to travel or to conduct a homeland attack. The foreign terrorist now has direct access into the United States like never before.

In recent arrests, a group of individuals was contacted by a known ISIL supporter who had already successfully traveled to Syria and encouraged them to do the same.

Some of these conversations occur in publicly accessed social networking sites, but others take place via private-messaging platforms. As a result, it is imperative the FBI and all law enforcement organizations understand the latest communication tools and are positioned to identify and prevent terror attacks in the homeland. We live in a technologically-driven society and just as private industry has adapted to modern forms of communication so too have the terrorists. Unfortunately, changing forms of internet communication are quickly outpacing laws and technology designed to allow for the lawful intercept of communication content. This real and growing gap the FBI refers to as ''Going Dark'' is the source of continuing focus for the FBI, it must be urgently addressed as the risks associated with ''Going Dark'' are grave both in traditional criminal matters as well as in National security matters. We are striving to ensure appropriate, lawful collection remains available. Whereas traditional voice telephone companies are required by CALEA to develop and maintain capabilities to intercept communications when law enforcement has lawful authority, that requirement does not extend to most internet communications services. As a result, such services are developed and deployed without any ability for law enforcement to collect information critical to criminal and National security investigations and prosecutions.

The FBI, in partnership with the Department of Homeland Security, is utilizing all lawful investigative techniques and methods to combat the threat these individuals may pose to the United States. In conjunction with our domestic and foreign partners, we are rigorously collecting and analyzing intelligence information as it pertains to the on-going threat posed by foreign terrorist organizations and homegrown violent extremists. In partnership with our many—Federal, State, and local agencies assigned to Joint Terrorism Task Forces around the country, we remain vigilant to ensure the safety of the American public. Be assured, the FBI continues to pursue increased efficiencies and information-sharing processes as well as pursue technological and other methods to help stay ahead of threats to the homeland.

Chairman McCaul, Ranking Member Thompson, and committee Members, I thank you for the opportunity to testify concerning terrorists' use of the internet and social media as a platform for spreading ISIL propaganda and inspiring individuals to target the homeland. I am happy to answer any questions you might have.

Chairman MCCAUL. Thank you, Director Steinbach.

I now recognize myself for 5 minutes.

I want to first pull up on the screen what I consider to be an internet conspiracy to conduct a terrorist attack. I was a Federal prosecutor, worked on drug cases, organized crime. There are a lot of similarities, but this one is conducted completely on the internet.

[The information follows:]

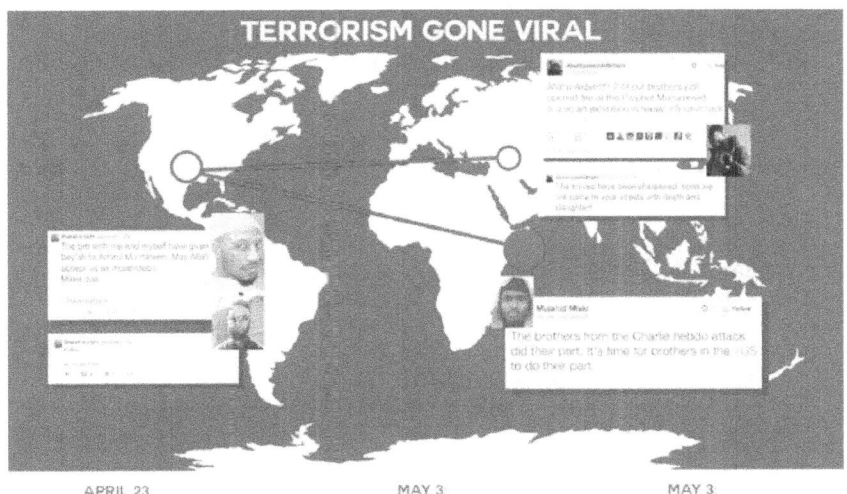

TERRORISM GONE VIRAL

APRIL 23	MAY 3	MAY 3
ISIS RECRUITER MISKI	GARLAND TERRORIST SIMPSON	TOP ISIS PROPAGANDIST HUSSAIN

Chairman McCaul. Let me first commend—I want to commend the FBI, Homeland Security, and the Joint Terrorism Task Forces for their textbook model case efforts in both the Garland attack, and most recently in Boston. That is the way it is supposed to work. Unfortunately, you have to get it right every time, and they just have to get it right once.

But this kind-of shows what we are dealing with the threat gone viral. You have this guy Miski, the ISIS follower in Somalia, directing attacks against the cartoonist art competition to Mr. Simpson, who responds, and as the attack is being conducted, we have the infamous Mr. al-Britani, who has become one of the chief ISIS recruiters, hackers, directors for terrorist attacks, congratulating them, basically saying: The knives have been sharpened; soon we will come to your streets with death and slaughter.

I guess my first question is to Director Steinbach. This is just a microcosm of the conspiracy on the internet that we are looking at and the threat that we are looking at on the internet.

How many potential recruiters do you think we have sitting in Syria and Somalia and northern Africa actively recruiting acts of terrorism globally?

Mr. Steinbach. That is a good question, sir. So I think you can refer to the Brookings Institute study on terrorists' use of social media, in particular Twitter, and it gives you an idea of what we are dealing with. So when you look at the volume of social media and its social—and its ability to spread horizontally, you probably look at a—in the neighborhood of a couple thousand core users, propagandists, that are pushing that message out, and then probably in the neighborhood of 50,000 based on the study that is in open source of individuals re-tweeting that message and then again upwards of 200,000, say, for instance, receiving that message. So that is our pool with which to start. Those are just, you know, ball-park numbers.

So, unfortunately, social media is a great tool for the public, but it also allows for this horizontal distribution, which is very difficult to follow. So those are baseline the numbers that we start with.

Chairman MCCAUL. Baseline you start with. You said—and it has been reported over as many as 200,000 pro-ISIS tweets per day occur on the internet. Is that correct?

Mr. STEINBACH. So I couldn't give you the exact numbers. It is a large volume, and that is the trick. Right? What is somebody's individual right to tweet and say what they want to say versus somebody who is going down a different road, a more nefarious road. So that is our starting point, is those thousands that you talk about in trying to cull through that and find out who amongst those individuals are up to no good, who amongst those individuals are potentially plotting an attack on Western interests.

Chairman MCCAUL. That is the great challenge that the FBI and Homeland has, is to try to, you know, monitor, to the extent you can, these communications.

Mr. STEINBACH. It is hugely problematic. So the social media is great. It is out there. It is open-source, but the volume is immense. That, of course, I am talking about the open side of social media. I am not talking about encrypted direct messaging, which is also a very problematic issue for us.

Chairman MCCAUL. How many of those followers are actually in the United States in your estimate?

Mr. STEINBACH. So I think Director Comey stated at last there is hundreds, maybe thousands. It is a challenge to get a full understanding of just how many of those passive followers are taking action.

Chairman MCCAUL. I have read some of these Twitter accounts and tweets. They have thousands of followers and thousands following, which means they are actively communicating and pinging each other, and then they go into—let's go into messaging. Then they go into a more secure space that if we have coverage we can pick up that communication, but as you suggested in your testimony, then they have the ability to go on to what is called dark space, to another platform that is secure comm that we don't have the ability to monitor these communications. Is that correct?

Mr. STEINBACH. That is correct, sir.

Chairman MCCAUL. To me, that is one of the greatest concerns I have. Do we have any idea how many communications are taking place in the dark space?

Mr. STEINBACH. No. We don't. That is the problem. We are past going dark in certain instances. We are dark. The ability to know what they are saying in these encrypted communication situations is troubling.

Chairman MCCAUL. I think it is a tremendous threat to the homeland. Do you have any recommendations for the Congress?

Mr. STEINBACH. I think we need to have an honest conversation. Get past the rhetoric of what we are talking about. We are not talking about large-scale surveillance techniques. We are talking about going before the court, whether the criminal court or the National security court with evidence, a burden of proof, probable cause, suggesting a crime has been committed, or in our case, that there is a terrorist, and showing that burden of proof, having the court sign off on it, and then going to those providers and requesting access to either that stored information or that communications that is on-going. So we are not looking at going through a back door or being nefarious. We are talking about going to the company and asking for their assistance. So we suggest and we are imploring Congress to help us seek legal remedies towards that, as well as asking companies to provide technological solutions to help that.

We understand privacy. Privacy, above all other things, including safety and freedom from terrorism is not where we want to go.

Chairman MCCAUL. Well, and I think this committee should be looking at this very important issue.

Finally, if you can't comment on the most recent Boston case, it has been reported that this was a ISIS-inspired event over the internet and an attempt to behead police officers. We know that a lot of their commands and call to arms are to attack military installations and attack police officers. I know you—it is an active investigation, but to the extent you can comment on this, would you please do so?

Mr. STEINBACH. Investigation is early on post-event. So there is not a lot I could say on the intelligence side. You are right, sir. We know that ISIL has put out a message to attack the West, specifically law enforcement, military. We know that they have been looking at those target sets. So we are very careful in where we are at. The targets that are out there, the counterterrorism subjects, we are monitoring them very closely for any type of action, any type of overt steps, any mobilization factors, and when we see those, we are not taking the chance.

Chairman MCCAUL. I appreciate that, and we again commend your efforts in this most recent threat.

With that, the Chairman now recognizes the Ranking Member.

Mr. THOMPSON. Thank you, Mr. Chairman.

Mr. Steinbach, you went into great detail the challenge of social media and other things. Do you at this point see the challenge also resources or the authority to do your job?

Mr. STEINBACH. I don't feel we have a challenge resource-wise. We have done an effective job identifying, prioritizing, and working through the JTTFs, the State, locals, to focus the target set. So I would say that of course we always have to prioritize resources, but it is more so the challenge for me is the technological challenge to get over that hurdle.

Mr. THOMPSON. When you said "technological," is it just—explain that a little bit for me, please.

Mr. STEINBACH. So when a company, a communications company or an ISP or a social media company, elects to build in its software encryption, end-to-end encryption, and leaves no ability for even the company to access that, we don't have the means by which to see the content. When we intercept it, we intercept encrypted communications. So that is the challenge, working with those companies to build technological solutions to prevent encryption above all else.

Mr. THOMPSON. So there is nothing from a Congressional standpoint authority you need from us to make that happen?

Mr. STEINBACH. Well, I think a number of years ago Congress passed CALEA, which was a law that was put in place that required telecommunication providers to provide assistance to law enforcement. I would suggest that that is a starting point that we need to expand who is bound by that law. Telecommunication providers are just a small subset of the companies that are out there that provide communication services these days. So I think it is a starting point that would be helpful.

Mr. THOMPSON. So can you provide the committee with beyond the starting point in terms of where the Department thinks we should be going in this direction?

Mr. STEINBACH. Sir, I could. I think more appropriately the FBI's OTD, the Operational Technology Division, has the lead on that, and they can—and I am sure they would be happy to come here and kind of lay out for you step-by-step where they need to go.

Mr. THOMPSON. I think, Mr. Chairman, we ought to try to make that part of what we do.

Chairman McCAUL. I agree.

Mr. THOMPSON. Okay.

Mr. Mulligan, according to your testimony, videos, tweets, and messages are probably not enough to radicalize individuals who are beginning to show these tendencies. They serve as discussion points. Showing interest and having on-line discussions are not criminal in nature. So what do we do about all these on-line portals that kind of start this—people down this slope, so to speak?

Mr. MULLIGAN. Sir, as my colleague mentioned, so it is part of a dialogue. They start out by trying to gain your interest. It is marketing and advertising. As Michael indicated, a lot of it is there is followers. You know, you frequently start out as following someone and following the trail, or you are subscribing to one of their channels. Then it progresses beyond that into a dialogue. So what we really need to be doing is helping educate a lot of the members of the public about this process. We have been trying to do that with DHS so that like, as Michael also said, family members are aware that if their children are spending a lot of time on this, they need to be able to counter that. They need to be able to execute some degree of measures.

These individuals are very savvy in their understanding of the gradual nature of recruitment and operationalization. So what they try to do is create a series of images that are attractive, and then they try and broaden that into a further discussion. So it does require, again, a much more active interventionist approach.

Mr. THOMPSON. General Taylor, can you kind of tell us where the DHS fits in this space in terms of trying to do the community engagement and some other kinds of things that can help what Mr. Mulligan is talking about?

Mr. TAYLOR. Yes, sir, certainly. As my colleagues on both sides have mentioned, it starts with the intelligence to understand the tactics, techniques, and procedures that our adversaries are using to reach into our communities, and we go out with NCTC, with the FBI, with the Department of Justice, to conduct community resilience exercises to teach communities about the tactics, techniques, and procedures, what to look for, how to spot it, who they may report to about that activity so that they can intervene at the earliest possible stage. We have done that across the country.

Secretary Johnson has done six of them so far this year. He is actually out doing one this afternoon. It is a clear part of our strategy to ensure the communities understand this threat and how it is being manifested. In my mind, it is almost like what we do with predatory behavior with child molesters in that we have got to inform parents of what is happening on the internet so that they can go and monitor what their children are doing and seeing on a continuous basis.

Mr. THOMPSON. Last question. Do parents who are monitoring, do they have enough options out there? You know, I think if a parent suspects that my child might be engaged in this behavior, you know, who do I call? Do I call the local law enforcement? Do I call the FBI? Or have I really put my child in a situation where I am labeling that child for life? Do we have anything in between law enforcement and the parent that can help mitigate some of these circumstances?

Mr. TAYLOR. Well, certainly I think the opportunity is for the community to engage, for the schools to engage before it gets to a radical action that requires law enforcement involvement. So what we try to get communities to understand is that they are a part of the solution and it is not just the law enforcement solution that we are looking for. We are looking for communities to be engaged, to understand, and to intervene when these events occur.

There is a recent case we had where a father in New England, his daughter went missing. He went to the airport in his State and said: I think my daughter is leaving. We were able to find his daughter—she wasn't at that airport; she was at another airport—before she got on a plane to go to overseas. That happens almost every day with somebody having that sort of challenge, and it is not a law enforcement response. It is helping parents be good parents and helping their children not make bad mistakes.

Mr. THOMPSON. Thank you, Mr. Chairman.

I yield back.

Chairman MCCAUL. Mr. King is recognized.

Mr. KING. Thank you, Mr. Chairman.

Let me thank all the witnesses for their testimony today and for the tremendous service they have given our country. So thank you very much.

I would just like to expand on something or maybe slightly disagree with something the Ranking Member said, and maybe it is more for the point of clarification, about whether or not ISIS' use of the social media can by itself cause someone to carry out violent action.

I know, in many cases, it may be part of a long process, but we had two recent cases in New York where there was a man in Jamaica, Queens, who attacked two police officers with a hatchet. It doesn't appear as if there was a long process of radicalization there. He was responding to, in effect, a directive from ISIS.

Then we had two women. Now, this may—somewhat a longer process, also in Queens, who had IEDs in their apartments. They both seemed to—primarily their means of radicalization was the ISIS' use of social media. Am I correct in that or—I think I am not trying to disagree with the Ranking Member. I just wanted to add on to that.

Mr. MULLIGAN. I would suggest, Congressman, that you are absolutely correct in their—they believe they are able to operationalize people solely through social media. They believe that they can enter into the dialogue I referred to earlier and provide the tools, and they are not getting into very complex tools.

What they are telling them is: Here are some tactics and procedures you should use. Here is some easily available—readily-available information on-line that you can exploit. In other words, they believe that they can provide them everything that they will need to undertake some kind of lone-actor attack.

Mr. STEINBACH. Let me add to that, sir. You also hit on an important point, and that is the diversity of the threat. You have got a slow burn, but you also have individuals who are flash to bang, which is very quick. We have seen more of this flash to bang with ISIL and their on-line efforts. Again, it is not just going someplace on the internet and looking it up. The social media push is coming right to your pocket via your smart phone. So it is a diversity of threats. So you are right in that it all depends on the individual. But we have to be prepared for both types of situations.

Mr. KING. I think you were very—all of you were eloquent as far as some of the dark areas, where you just can't go right now. It would seem to me that in those instances, it is even more important to have human sources on the ground that can fill in those gaps. I would just say, and maybe this is rhetorical on my part, but with the constant criticism of law enforcement and the constant talk of snooping and spying, for instance, to me it makes it much harder to recruit people on the ground. Like in Boston, if this had been 2 days ago, and the Associated Press and the *New York Times* uncovered the fact that the Boston Police were following those alleged terrorists, that would have been snooping and spying. Well, now it turns out, after the fact, it was effective surveillance. I just think that the use of those terms really are doing a tremendous disservice as far as enabling law enforcement to recruit people on the ground. You said you want to work with the community, and you do, but at the same time this onslaught coming from the media and from certain people in politics, constantly talking about snooping, spying, harassment, to me, it undoes a lot of the good that you are trying to do. So I don't know if you want to comment or not. Again, maybe I was just making a rhetorical point. But if anyone wishes to comment, fine. If not I will just——

Mr. STEINBACH. I agree with you, sir. You have to have a multitude of tripwires, both on-line and in person. We try to insert sources in situations where there is a predicated investigation, but it is a challenge.

Mr. TAYLOR. Sir, I would add to what Mr. Steinbach has said and indicate that this is a total team fight. It takes HUMINT. It takes SIGINT. It takes what I call transaction INT, looking at travel patterns and those sorts of things to come to this. Certainly in communities, communities sometimes feel: Well, you are looking at us too much as opposed to another community. Our response is generally: The bad guys are trying to recruit your kids. That is why we are talking to you. It is not because of your religion, but it is what the bad guys are trying do. That is why we are here talking to you about strategies to defend yourself.

Mr. KING. My time is running out. Just if you could comment on this. ISIS, one thing they have been doing it appears is encouraging use of hoax threats. Are you in a position it say yet whether or not what happened on Memorial Day, with 10 different hoax threats were called into the airlines and again this weekend when they were called in, if that is in response to ISIS? Are these lone wolves? Or is it just a person carrying out a hoax?

Mr. STEINBACH. I would say we don't have any credible information that there are threats to aviation right now. So, yes, the ones so far appear to be hoaxes. Tracking those back to an individual or a group is still an on-going process.

Mr. KING. But ISIS has said that the use of the hoax itself is an effective means of attack.

Mr. STEINBACH. Correct. Correct.

Mr. KING. I yield back. Thank you, Mr. Chairman.

Thank you for your testimony.

Chairman MCCAUL. Mr. Richmond is recognized.

Mr. RICHMOND. I guess I will start with you, Mr. Taylor, or maybe even Mr. Mulligan. You mentioned that there were about 1,700 messages sent out by ISIL. How many, if you had to estimate, about how many people did that reach?

Mr. MULLIGAN. Certainly tens of thousands; 1,700 separate publications, be it a video release or an on-line magazine release, but certainly in the thousands to tens of thousands probably.

Mr. RICHMOND. The people who start to follow and engage in the social media, even if it is on the front, we are not seeing any similarities or any consistent traits across the board in the people that start to engage, or are we?

Mr. MULLIGAN. Well, sir, it is partly about what the actual publication is or the video is about or what they are trying to incite. In some instances, as you know, we are particularly concerned when we see someone who is let's say a Twitter feed that is being followed and they are really strongly advocating violence. Then I think the FBI is paying particular attention to those. It is important to also note that in some instances a lot of the followers are just—I mean, they are paying attention. The media is paying attention to some of these entities. On a lot of the video releases, obviously, they are tracking and reporting on it.

I would also like to posit that, in many instances, they are also trying to generate buzz themselves. So we have seen multiple instances in which they have, if you will, collaborators who will retweet messages to try and increase the numbers so that it makes it look like they have got a very large number of followers. The bottom line is they are effective at using social media, and they are effective at, if you will, manipulating social media.

Mr. RICHMOND. Knowing that they are experts at manipulating social media and using social media, are there things that we can do or things that we should encourage others to do or not to do to protect themselves? I guess now I am going to get into the sensitive area of, you know, I am not commenting whether it is their First Amendment right to have a contest to depict or make fun of Islam. But in my mind, I encourage my mother not to walk down dark streets at night because it is dangerous. I would get upset if some-one drew cartoons of Jesus or called Mary a slut. I mean, that is just my faith.

So if you know they are social media experts and they are good at using social media to get their message out, are we inciting some of this with our or some people's hatred towards their religion and other things? I mean, are we fueling some of this fight?

Mr. TAYLOR. Sir, I think I would answer that question simply by saying the Constitution of the United States of America and our rights and freedoms are something that stands in the way of our enemies' effort to create a global caliphate. So I don't think any one event fuels this. I think it is coming at our system of government; our freedoms is what they are trying to undermine. They are in the news cycle.

Mr. RICHMOND. So you don't see any spike in people following after events like this or any rise in social media conversations when you have a contest like that going on?

Mr. TAYLOR. Of course, you do.

Mr. RICHMOND. I guess that is my question then.

Mr. TAYLOR. But, again, in America, those kinds of conversations happen every day as a part of our Constitutional rights in this country. So saying that we should stop doing something here would cause them to stop doing it there, they will find somewhere else to look for a reason to, you know, to attack America.

Mr. RICHMOND. I agree with that.

But I guess my question is, and I think that a guy that is going to rob a lady walking down a dark alley is going to rob somebody. But I am going to encourage my mother not to walk down that alley so it won't be her so that it is not easy prey.

I guess, you know, it is our Constitutional right to say whatever you want. But I promise you if you call my mother a bad name, there are going to be some consequences and repercussions. I just don't think that we are having that honest conversation. When we are talking about young people, we are talking about angry people, we are talking about people who feel picked on.

I mean, you know, there are some words that will trigger a re-sponse, but you have the absolute First Amendment right to say it. Then it is up to me whether I want to exercise my discipline or hit you in the mouth. So the question becomes: How often are we going to get hit in the mouth before we realize that we may be playing into it unnecessarily by just being callous and cruel I think in some instances?

Thank you for your questions.

Thank you, Mr. Chairman.

Chairman MCCAUL. I thank the gentleman.

Mr. Perry is recognized.

Mr. PERRY. Thank you, Mr. Chairman.

Thank you gentlemen for being here.

I think this is a difficult subject, trying to find the line between privacy and security, as I think everybody has alluded to. Let me ask you this.

There are folks that might wear their heart on their sleeve re-garding this circumstance, radical Islam, attacks, and so on and so forth. They might be having a conversation openly on social media where they espouse their opinions, which might lead them to be a target for some of these individuals, if you know what I mean, and maybe even some of the folks in this building, somebody that is having this hearing today or somebody that is asking questions like this.

Do you folks have any way or do the platforms have any way of monitoring traffic about those individuals that might have had a conversation with a friend openly on open source, on-line, about their disdain for radical Islam, for attacks, and might have been disparaging about it? Do they become a target? Does that individual become a target? Is there any way that the social platforms have a way of monitoring it? Do any of you folks have a way of monitoring it? Do you collaborate on that?

Is that a chill? Is there a chilling effect for free speech if people feel like they might be targeted because of their thoughts posted openly on social media?

Mr. STEINBACH. So I am not sure that I fully understand the question. So I think that social media platforms usually abide by the terms of service agreement. They have got small compliance departments. For the most part, the answer to the first part, no, I don't think social media companies are doing anything along the lines that you speak.

As far as the intelligence community or law enforcement monitoring those individuals who are exercising expressions of freedom and then become targets, we don't have a mechanism in place to track them. We would track it from the other side if we see threats coming toward them. But not necessarily—is that the question you are asking, sir?

Mr. PERRY. Essentially, yeah.

Mr. STEINBACH. So we are not tracking it from the other end.

Now if somebody comes to us and says, "Hey, I feel threatened," of course we will look into that. But as far as a data pull of some type of large scale to look at that, no.

Mr. PERRY. Go ahead.

Mr. MULLIGAN. If I could also offer another bit of context to what Mike said. When you are operating on social media, particularly some of the broadly-available public platforms, you are in open space. So you can be monitored by any entity out there, by commercial entities, by educational institutions, by the media. Anyone can be looking at that. That is one of the challenges that I think people are often concerned about, going back to this point that you make.

Frequently within this country we are trying to—I mean, trying to encourage credible voices to contest the ideological extremism that is being advocated. Those folks are often reluctant to do so because of the fact that they are concerned that they will either, as you said, become a potential target of violence, become an intelligence target, become a law enforcement target.

I think what we have been trying to do collectively as a community is trying to change that environment, at least from the perception of the U.S. Government's monitoring of their activities. But I do believe that, again, it is open space. So any person that enters into that space needs to understand that.

Mr. PERRY. So when you talk about—some of you talked about encrypted direct messages and dark space. Can you give me some examples? Is it essentially just texting? Would that be considered off limits to monitoring by the United States Government even in cases where there might be an imminent planning and plotting? Is there any way—and if this is Classified, that is fine, too. But I am just wondering from that perspective, you know, if it is not on Facebook, if it is not on Twitter, do we have the capability—the Federal Government, do they have the capability and/or do the providers have the capability? Are there algorithms that pick this type of stuff up or processes that pick this stuff up?

Mr. STEINBACH. The answer is no. There are 200-plus social media companies. Some of these companies build their business model around end-to-end encryption. There is no ability currently for us to see that. So if we intercept the communication, all we see is encrypted communication.

Mr. PERRY. Anybody else? Some examples. Are we talking just straight texting? Like I know a program called Cyber Dust, right? So once you send it and it is received, it disappears. That would be—is that an example of the dark space, or is that just encrypted direct communications? What is that?

Mr. STEINBACH. So dark space is a general term. So, yes, there is lots of models out there. There is models in social media that go point-to-point and then once you read it, it disappears; it is not saved. Some companies can set, you can set how long a text is saved. Some of them are encrypted from the start. Most of them are text-type direct forms. Some of them are photographs that send. There is all kinds of different models. Some of them are more like bulletin board formats. There is lot and lots of formats out there.

Mr. PERRY. All that is off-limits right now to the Federal Government as far as you are——

Mr. STEINBACH. It is not that it is off-limits. It is that there are more and more of these companies are building their platforms that don't allow us. We will still seek to—they will go to those companies and serve them legal process, but if the company has built a model that even they can't decrypt, then it doesn't do us any good.

Mr. PERRY. Thank you, Mr. Chairman.

I yield back.

Chairman MCCAUL. Mrs. Watson Coleman is recognized.

Mrs. WATSON COLEMAN. Thank you very much, Mr. Chairman.

Thank you very much, gentlemen, for your information sharing here. I think I want to tag on a little bit to Congressman Richmond's questions because I want to get at something that I have not heard a lot about.

I am reading that there really is no sort-of common denominator here, not any religious zealot. Individuals who are being radicalized don't even necessarily know what the Islam religion is all about. It is not socioeconomic. It is not racial or ethnic.

So I am trying to figure out what exactly is it? What is enticing about beheadings and violence and this just very angry assault that our young people are being exposed to? What is tripping them and their attention to that kind of radicalization? What is it about ISIL?

Mr. MULLIGAN. So, ma'am, if I can just give you a little bit of context on that. You are right to describe—and I think one of my colleagues described earlier—the range of how can I say it, experiences and, if you will, ideological knowledge, religious knowledge varies incredibly widely. What there seems to be is, they are appealing in some instances to, if there is a sense of victimization, that they are the individuals who are those who, you know, will conquer those who have been the victimizers. So it appeals to that, to that underdog nature. They really do an effective job in communicating that sense.

As I said in my remarks, they couple that with an ability to present: Here is the idealized vision of what our religion presents. If you really want to leave the trappings of all the challenges and troubles you are having in your current life and join us, we will offer you more direction and more means. So that is how they seem to be succeeding.

Mrs. WATSON COLEMAN. So they seem to be attracting young people. Are we talking about middle school age? Are we talking— what ages are we talking about? When we say ''youth,'' just how young are these young people?

Mr. MULLIGAN. I would say we are seeing ages in the teens, probably upper teens into 20s. It is also important, you know, we deem this a new generation of terrorists because as General Taylor was saying, a lot of them are extremely conversant in a lot of social media. I mean they have grown up with it. So this is the means by which they use to reach that generation.

Mrs. WATSON COLEMAN. I can understand that. What I don't understand is what is enticing them. What appeals to you when you see someone beheaded or you see these nasty threats or you see this violence? The victimization is something I would like to just carry on a little bit. One of my favorite programs was about the FBI profiler. So I am wondering, is that a real thing? I know there is police profiling I am concerned about. But is there such a thing as psychological profiling? Are we looking at those kinds of things? Are we identifying some traits that have nothing to do with ethnicity or socioeconomic or whatever, but other traits? Are we able to like identify any sort of red flags in the children and the young people in school and in college? Because I just wonder whether or not we are expending enough energy and resources in trying to identify early on and intervene.

Mr. STEINBACH. So, yes, the FBI does have a Behavioral Analysis Unit. There is within the National Center for the Analysis of Violent Crime, there is a unit dedicated to terrorists. It spends a lot of time looking at the parts of radicalization and mobilization, what attracts folks. But like Mr. Mulligan said, it is a very complicated piece.

Quite frankly, what we have seen as far as a profile is the lack of a profile. There is just so many reasons. You know, we don't see disaffected. We see some disaffected. We don't see well-to-do. We see some well-to-do. Victimization is certainly a common theme. Younger and younger individuals are drawn into this messaging. I would say that ISIL has done an effective message versus al-Qaeda in that they have said publicly: Hey, the caliphate is here today.

You can come now to a country where sharia law rules. Bring your family.

They have really messaged it across the spectrum to a wide walk of individuals.

Mrs. WATSON COLEMAN. Let me just ask this last question, if I might: Should we be engaging the Department of Education, higher education, in identifying programs and approaches and sort-of learning devices that would be able to anticipate and deal with our younger people who are affected by whatever it is that is turning them on here?

Mr. TAYLOR. Yes, ma'am, we should, and we are beginning to work with the Department of Education on these kinds of issues because it is a whole-of-community effort. It is not just the police, not just the churches. But it is education. It is civic organizations as well.

Mrs. WATSON COLEMAN. Thank you, Mr. Chairman.

At some point, I really would like for us to explore what more can be done proactively in identifying and sort-of intervening at an earlier stage.

Thank you for your indulgence.

Chairman McCAUL. Thank you.

Mr. Hurd is recognized.

Mr. HURD. Thank you, Mr. Chairman and Ranking Member, for holding this hearing. I think a number of these issues we can talk all day long about that, and so we are packing a lot in in a very short period of time.

My first question is to Mr. Mulligan and Ambassador Taylor. Talk about the community engagement exercises and engaging credible voices throughout these communities. How do we blow that up? How do we make it bigger? How do we accelerate those projects?

Mr. MULLIGAN. So we have been developing a partnership community awareness briefing, and we have just been moving it out fairly slowly initially to ensure that we are having a degree of success. But we have had some success in that. Now we are trying to train the trainer so that we can get into a situation where we are propagating it more broadly across the communities. Because going back to some of the other observations that have been made, it really is at the community level that we need to have this success. Also we need to have, I think as the Ranking Member said, levels between Government and local. In a lot of instances, particularly with family members, as you know, people are reluctant to engage any sort of authorities. We need to try and find that middle ground, sir.

Mr. HURD. I appreciate that. Because we need to be thinking about this in terms of weeks, not years. Because that is the speed at which we need to counter this threat. Ambassador Taylor, do you have any remarks on that?

Mr. TAYLOR. It is a global phenomenon. So our outreach internationally has been important as well. I am leading a delegation to Australia next week to further our communication with our Five Eyes partners about this phenomenon and how we can engage communities really across the world so they better understand what this risk threat is.

Mr. HURD. Because in order to make the FBI's job a lot easier, this lone-wolf idea, the way we are going to stop that is by countering that violent ideology and extremist ideology. That is going to take a whole-of-Government effort. Who in the Government is responsible for this? The CVE activity.

Mr. TAYLOR. It is actually a shared responsibility between Justice, the intelligence community, DHS, and the FBI. Our deputies meet regularly to formulate those strategies and to implement those strategies within the United States.

Mr. HURD. My suggestion there would be looking at unity of commands because when you have three people in charge of something, nobody is in charge of it. I think that is something that we are plagued with in the Federal Government on a number of occasions. My next set of questions is to Mr. Steinbach.

The canon out there on counterterrorism is clear, terrorists are trying do two things: They are trying to kill a lot of people, and they are trying to elicit counterterrorism responses in a government to upset a population to foment discord. All right. So with that as the background, that is why I am a little bit nervous when we start talking about CALEA expansion, all these kinds of things, I get nervous because of the privacy aspect.

So my question, and not to get too technical, does end-to-end encryption that is provided by many U.S. companies prevent your ability to do attribution?

Mr. STEINBACH. In some cases, yes.

Mr. HURD. But not in all cases?

Mr. STEINBACH. Not in all cases.

Mr. HURD. All right. So are you suggesting that when you have a court order on someone connected to terrorism that there are companies that aren't cooperating with helping to get as much information as they can about that individual?

Mr. STEINBACH. No. What I am suggesting is that companies have built a product that doesn't allow them to help.

Mr. HURD. But if you are saying it doesn't prevent attribution—because the key here is to try to find as much information so that we can—you know, to exhibit the success that you all have had in Boston. You know, you were able to identify someone and use other tools to track him and stop and prevent this from happening. That is, you know, it is a difficult task. Don't get me wrong. I know how hard you guys are working. Maintaining the operational pace that you all have maintained since September 11 is unprecedented. Your men and women in the FBI should be patted on the back and heralded. But we also got to make sure that we are protecting our civil liberties and our borders at the same time. When you talk about reviewing applicable laws around the technology challenges that you are facing in CALEA expansion, I just want to be clear you are not talking about putting a back door in software, are you?

Mr. STEINBACH. No. Like I said in my prepared statement, sir, I am talking about full transparency. I am talking about going to the companies who then could help us get the unencrypted information. The attribution piece is important to understand that, depending on the technology involved—and this requires, quite frankly, a technology discussion—there are tokens that are used that do not allow for attribution. So it is not quite as simple as just using other techniques or attributions, sometimes that attribution is not there. I would be happy to discuss in a Classified setting in more detail just exactly what we are talking about.

Mr. HURD. I would love that. Thank you.

One thing, we have been talking a lot about the use of social media and digital tools and how it has made it easier for ISIS to recruit people. But it also gives us an opportunity to do double-agent operations against them, to penetrate, you know, their ability. When chasing al-Qaeda, you know, 10 years ago, if you were anything close to an American, you would get your throat slit. Now we have these new tools in order to penetrate them. Again, I know I have run out of time.

I yield back that to the Chairman. Thank you.

Chairman MCCAUL. If I could just briefly comment, we led a delegation on investigating foreign fighters to the Middle East and Europe. We found that there is a counternarrative out there. This is more not on-line, but foreign fighters who have left the region, some returned inspired and more radicalized, and some returned very disillusioned from the experience. I think that narrative, and this may be more a State Department issue, the more we get that narrative out there, the better off we are going to be.

The Chairman recognizes Miss Rice.

Miss RICE. Thank you, Mr. Chairman.

Mr. Steinbach, I just want to ask you a couple of questions. How does the intelligence community qualify an elevated threat from on-line-inspired terrorists? So we all know how when they raise the threat level, but specifically with this on-line communication, how do you rate what the—what level the communication, how it rises to something that you really are worried about?

Mr. STEINBACH. So it is I think a simple question with a complicated answer. There is lots of pieces. The volume, the specificity, whether or not they have identified willing sympathizers who will do something. It is a lot of pieces that go into it. Many of those factors are present now.

Miss RICE. So are there any difficulties? What is the biggest difficulty in terms of being accurate when you are trying to rate the level of a threat?

Mr. STEINBACH. So as Mr. Hurd stated previously, the social media is great because it is out-there social media—it is voluminous, but it is volume. So there is trying to weed through the thousands and thousands of individuals on social media and find the—all the noise out there, identifying the signals. So it is a volume piece. You know, looking at social media requires a different business process that we do things with, and going from there to finding a credible threat, it is a very difficult process.

Miss RICE. I mean, it seems like it would be. We have been talking this whole time about on-line communications, on-line radicalization. Is there any physical presence of either ISIL or al-Qaeda doing face-to-face recruiting here in this country?

Mr. STEINBACH. So I would say we don't—we have, of course, a number, a small number of returned foreign fighters. We have individuals who have been overseas and returned to the United States. Where they are and who they are is probably an intelligence gap for us. I would say our best estimates are we don't have ISIL sitting in the United States. We have got individuals who have taken up the call to arms based on ISIL's messaging.

Miss RICE. Right. But not everyone who has gone and come back becomes a recruiter. So I am just curious as to whether there are people who don't go anywhere, aren't on the internet and are actually in a physical place actually doing, you know, whether in tandem with the on-line recruitment actual face-to-face recruiting.

Mr. STEINBACH. So you are talking about a classical home-grown violent extremist, the lone wolf. There are a number of factors that would cause somebody to radicalize. It doesn't have to be on-line. It could be a friend, an associate. Other factors may cause that person to become radicalized. On-line just happens to be, when you look at the spectrum, by volume, the highest percentage.

If you are asking, do we have core al-Qaeda coming to the United States and sitting here—or core ISIL, I think we look at that intelligence gap all the time. But I would say, for the most part, no.

Miss RICE. Okay. Thank you.

I yield back my time. Thank you, Mr. Chairman.

Chairman MCCAUL. Mr. Duncan is recognized.

Mr. DUNCAN. Thank you, Mr. Chairman.

Al-Qaeda led the way with *Inspire* magazine, I think, which was an on-line publication. Are we still seeing *Inspire* as prevalent as it was? Has ISIL adopted that media? Is there a way to track? You have got a website platform like *Inspire,* is there a way for you guys to track who visits that page, who takes it and forwards that information? If you can answer that for me.

Mr. MULLIGAN. Sir, to answer your question, *Inspire* still comes out periodically. That model has been successfully copied by several of the other affiliates and other terrorist-related entities. They see that whole process of like an on-line magazine as being an effective model. It has been adapted by ISIL. They have a publication called *Dabiq.* It is a variation on that. They put out their information. They put it out in multiple languages.

To answer your question about our ability to track its propagation, we are not really able to do that. They put multiple links to it. I mean, as you can imagine, once something starts to propagate on the internet, it is there. It can reside in a number of places. So that model does exist. It continues. They are continuing to employ it. Again, it is extremely difficult, impossible to track really.

Mr. DUNCAN. For the freshman Members and the people that just started following this issue, I would recommend that you get the *Inspire* magazine, take a look at some of the information that is being provided. I have never seen the information you are talking about that ISIL or others. If there is a way to share that with the committee, even if it is a Classified setting, we would be glad to take a look at that. I personally would like to do that.

I am very interested in the foreign fighter flow. I went last year to Europe to really delve into these foreign fighters coming off the battlefield from Syria, whether they transited through Turkey. When I was there, or right before I got to Brussels, a foreign fighter actually came back, shot up the museum there, the Jewish museum, killed three or four people, and tried to flee to north Africa through France. So the timeliness of my travels. But this was the very beginning; you didn't hear about ISIS as much in May and

June of last year, not like you hear about them now and at least over the last 12 months.

At the time, that foreign fighter that shot up the museum in Brussels, Germany knew, apparently knew, about him and failed to let the Belgians know or the French know because they were suspicious of U.S. intelligence gathering through monitoring phone calls and all that has come out after Snowden. So what are some of the challenges of tracking these foreign fighters? You talk about core al-Qaeda and core ISIL. I am talking about the fringe guys that go over and maybe get radicalized on the battlefield and decide: You know what? I can do this back home. How do we track those guys and how successful have we been?

Mr. MULLIGAN. So that has been, ironically, that has been an incredibly unifying factor among the counterterrorism community across the globe. A lot of our Western partners, so, I mean, they have got substantial foreign fighter flow issues. You know, as Mike indicated——

Mr. DUNCAN. Schengen region in Europe, you get there——

Mr. MULLIGAN. Yes, sir. Again, that is something they are trying to confront in Europe with regard to how do this they manage this with the Schengen flows right now? We have been sharing a lot of information back and forth with some of the means and processes that we are trying to employ to track foreign fighters. What is also very clear to us is it needs to be, particularly with our foreign partners, a whole-of-Government approach. We are trying to share with them the benefits that we have experienced by ensuring that the free flow of information among the interagency. In many instances, we will develop an effective relationship with a foreign partner, only to discover that the partner flow within their own nation is not optimized to try and ensure that appropriate law enforcement authorities have been alerted to that foreign fighter flow.

Mr. DUNCAN. Right.

Mr. MULLIGAN. But the bottom line is things are trending positively in the information sharing.

Mr. DUNCAN. Bilateral trade.

Mr. MULLIGAN. Multilateral, multilateral, sir. But the other challenge is, again, so we estimate there have been about 4,000 in total foreign fighters flowing from the West. But what we have seen is, again, there are foreign fighters from over a hundred countries. Some of our other partners, folks who are in that region, have developed very effective mechanisms for both tracking the foreign fighters and developing rehabilitation programs. So going back to some points that the general made earlier, we really need to do a lot of information sharing about their experiences at rehabilitation, their experiences at tracking, and incorporating them into some of our own processes.

Mr. DUNCAN. In the essence of time, north Africans are trying to get across the Med into Italy and Spain. Once they do, they have got pretty much free travel throughout Europe. So how do you target those? I mean, these are migrants that are getting on boats and coming across. We don't know about.

Mr. MULLIGAN. Interestingly, some of the direction that has been given lately, over the last several months by ISIL leadership, is they are urging a lot of these fighters to remain in place, to, as you know, they have been trying to establish branches of the caliphate in other countries. So they are trying to say: Hey, don't move. You don't need to move across north Africa. Stay in Libya and work with our branch there. So that is one other part of their strategy. That is how they are trying to offset that limitation.

Mr. TAYLOR. Sir, if I might add, we are working very closely with our European partners on that flow from Italy and into the northern parts of Europe. It is a very big concern for us, not only from a counterterrorism perspective, because eventually some of these people might end up applying for visas in our country. So it is a high priority for our intelligence exchanges with our partners in Europe in terms of getting our arms around that particular flow.

Mr. DUNCAN. All right. Thank you. I am out of time. Mr. Chairman, I would ask that we delve into the effectiveness of JTTFs with regard to some of this.

That might have to be in a Classified setting. But I yield back.

Chairman MCCAUL. Let me just say for the Members, we do have a do have Classified briefs with the FBI and Homeland, social media monitoring and on encryption challenges. JTTFs would be ripe. The other flaw I noticed in my travels is that European partners don't screen E.U. citizens past any watch list as they fly from, say, Istanbul back into Europe. I think that is a big security gap. We urged them to change that. I know the E.U. Parliament is addressing a change in their law.

Mr. TAYLOR. It is in work. It is not moving as fast as we would like it to move. But there are some glimmers of hope that based upon the recent activity, threats, and actions in Europe, that the Europeans understand the importance of PNR and other sorts of data tracking of citizens internal to the European Union. So we have some hope that there will be a light at the end of the tunnel going forward on that.

Chairman MCCAUL. I did as well.

Mr. Langevin.

Mr. LANGEVIN. Thank you. Mr. Chairman.

I want to thank our panel for their testimony here today. I apologize if any of the questions I am going to touch on have already been asked. I had to leave briefly to take a call from our commanding general in Afghanistan to get an update, a briefing on current status of things over there in my Armed Services Committee role. If I could begin with this. As some of you may know, I spent a lot of time and am very concerned about cybersecurity issues, particularly as they relate to critical infrastructure. Can you tell me in your role with respect to seeing this stepped-up effort using social media in recruitment and using cyber as a tool what you are seeing in terms of recruitment or efforts to use cyber weapons to attack critical infrastructure? Can you also describe what measures, if any, that are also different when combating the threat of a home-grown terrorist interested in cyberterrorism rather than more traditional physical attacks?

Mr. STEINBACH. Sir, I think it is a great question. I think, first of all, we are seeing more and more a blended threat, the cyber intrusion peace with the counterterrorism piece. Where we are at now, we do see those same terrorist actors using cyber intrusion as a tool. They are experimenting with it, seeing how effective they are. We have seen most recently in the last less than a year them becoming more and more adept at cyber intrusion-type activities.

Mr. TAYLOR. Sir, I would add to Mr. Steinbach's comments by saying that this is a very high-priority concern for the Department of Homeland Security, our National Protection and Programs Directorate work with the critical infrastructure community every day across this country about the cyber threat in general, and specifically about the threat from terrorist actors so that they are prepared for and understand the potential for that threat and have means of mitigating those sorts of attempts within our critical infrastructure.

Mr. LANGEVIN. Mr. Mulligan, do you have anything to add?

Mr. MULLIGAN. Yes, sir. I mean, I would agree with those points. I would also posit, again, it seems that it is an inevitable kind of trend that they would move into that realm. They would move into that realm because, again, it is a means by which they could effect damage in a very cost-efficient way. They are operating largely, they have a high degree of maneuverability in cyber space. So it seems quite logical that they would attempt to pursue that. We need to be developing mechanisms for detection of those activities, sir.

Mr. LANGEVIN. Have you seen those stepped-up efforts to specifically focus on that as a tool right now to be used to go operational?

Mr. STEINBACH. Yes. We have seen stepped-up efforts.

Mr. LANGEVIN. Okay. Thank you.

Mr. Mulligan, if I could turn to you, I am very supportive of efforts to incorporate counter-messaging into CVE strategies and the use of public-private partnerships, such as the Peer2Peer program that you mentioned in your testimony, to ensure these messages are heard.

At the same time, central to any effective counter-messaging strategy, though, is the credibility of the messenger, which can be greatly undermined if Government is involved. So how can we ensure that there are independent voices that can counter extremist messages without compromising the independence that gives their statements weight?

Mr. MULLIGAN. Sir, that is exactly some of the outreach efforts that we are trying to make with regard to the community advising piece. It is also—I mean, it is a question of establishing processes by which people will be able to feel free that they are able to have the tools to do that kind of counter-messaging. The challenges that we have, again, is there are still trust deficits that need to be overcome. We all, as you said, we need to find those intermediaries who are willing to take up that effort.

Mr. LANGEVIN. Thank you. For the panel and before my time runs out, social media platforms play a prominent role in all of your testimony, obviously. Can you describe the relationships that each of your agencies has with the private operators of these networks? Are these relationships institutional or more based on personal relationships? What kinds of requests do you make of these companies?

Mr. STEINBACH. So I won't get into specifics, sir. I would say that we have relationships with every company that is in that environment because we have to. We have to serve them process. It is based on personal relationships as a starting point, but we develop more than that. But I think each company is different. I don't think it is appropriate in this setting to talk about those particulars with that company.

Mr. TAYLOR. Sir, I would add that Homeland Security in our cybersecurity role has relationships with all of these companies. As Mr. Steinbach mentioned, we probably would want to have the conversation in a Classified environment.

Mr. LANGEVIN. Well, hopefully, we can perhaps follow up on that, Mr. Chairman, at a later date then.

Chairman McCAUL. Yeah. If I could just quickly follow up, a lot of people ask me why don't we conduct a cyber offensive attack to shut down these in the social media program. I guess the two problems with that is they will—you know, once that is done, they will open up another account rather quickly. No. 2, I guess our intelligence-gathering capability goes down quite a bit. You don't have to comment at all on that.

But the Chairman now recognizes Mr. Ratcliffe.

Mr. RATCLIFFE. Thank you, Mr. Chairman.

I want to thank you and the Ranking Member for holding this critically important hearing. Of course, I thank all the witnesses for being here today and for all the important work that you do every day to serve our country.

This attack in Garland really seems to underscore and demonstrate the unique challenges that ISIS is posing today. In Garland, we saw two dead terrorists and no civilian casualties. We saw law enforcement do exactly what they should have done, which is protect the public. Yet we are living in unprecedented times where a failed attack by ISIS in that regard is still spun as a win, where a failed attempt still plays into the narrative that they want to sell.

As a former terrorism prosecutor who handled a number of matters involving al-Qaeda, I have noticed something that appears to me to be an important difference. I want to ask you about that. You know, al-Qaeda and ISIS have both been encouraging lonewolf attacks, but al-Qaeda has been doing it for years with very little success. It seems to me that ISIS has been very effective in this regard in just a matter of months. We are at a situation, it appears to me, that ISIS' sophisticated use of social media is essentially having a cascading effect, if you will, where it has become a terrorism multiplier of sorts, one where lone-wolf attackers like Mr. Simpson or Mr. Soofi or Mr. Rahim can essentially use the ISIS brand without having to join ISIS.

In that regard, it concerns me that it would appear that ISIS has essentially created a terror franchise. So I want to very quickly ask you each whether you think I am accurate in that assessment.

Mr. MULLIGAN. Congressman, I think that is an excellent characterization. I would agree with you. That is precisely. They have very effectively leveraged that capability. They have exceptional capabilities. They claim they are making maximum use of every opportunity to amplify effect. You have seen them using it in terms of representing their victories on the battlefield and the way that they have obviously treated our hostages. They attempt to squeeze every bit of, if you will, perceptual power out of social media.

Mr. TAYLOR. I would agree with Mr. Mulligan in that regard.

I have been doing this for a long time, about 45 years. I have never seen a terrorist organization with the kind of public relations savvy that I have seen with ISIL globally. They have been very effective in using it.

Mr. STEINBACH. Yeah, I think my colleagues hit the main points. I would just add to that in addition that it is a focus on a Western audience. When you look at the social media tweets in English versus al-Qaeda or others, they are at a much higher rate. So it is a great propaganda message. It is a propaganda message that is focused on a Western English-speaking audience.

Mr. RATCLIFFE. So we are talking a lot about the effect of their message. I want to focus a little bit more on the cause.

Director Steinbach, you and the deputy director both talked about this, this sort-of unique narrative that ISIS has created, a false narrative, one that involves a sense of community, a sense of adventure, maybe the ability to find a spouse. We all know how ridiculous these claims are. But for those that are susceptible to radicalization, it seems to be an increasingly successful narrative from their standpoint. I am curious, since ISIS grew out of al-Qaeda in Iraq, why did ISIS suddenly become effective at crafting this message when al-Qaeda and other terrorist organizations really hadn't been previously? Do we have any insight into that?

Mr. MULLIGAN. I don't want to oversimplify it, but I would point out the demographic. They have attracted a younger generation of fighters who are much more conversant. They are in a situation where they have initially occupied territory in which there was fairly advanced infrastructure that could then be leveraged. So, I mean, if you think over time, as you know, al-Qaeda has, in some instances, they were not occupying optimal areas to try and leverage that infrastructure whereas ISIS did position itself very, very well. I also think they have a fundamental orientation to action that kind of dominates a lot of their psyche and how they move.

Mr. TAYLOR. I think the other difference, sir, is that social media wasn't as robust when al-Qaeda started as it has been since, actually since 2010, the Arab Spring, and how social media was used in those events and how it has propagated its use by other groups since that time.

Mr. STEINBACH. Just to further clarify what Frank said, he is absolutely right. So when you look at the internet, 4, 5, 6 years ago, it was anonymous, but you still, the bad guy, the individual living in the United States still had to reach to a forum, identify that forum, go into that forum.

With social media, it is pushed to you. It is so far advanced in comparison to the anonymous internet.

Mr. RATCLIFFE. My time has expired. I hope the Chairman will indulge me to ask one additional question. Because I think what is important here is I want to find out what the——we have talked about their effective messaging and the fact that they have created essentially a winning brand that is that is drawing the disaffected and disenfranchised to them. What are we doing to counter that message? What can we do besides——in other words, to create a losing brand for them? I realize that part of that is kinetic military operations on the ground. But from a social media standpoint, is there a counterstrategy?

Mr. MULLIGAN. So I would posit to you that there is basically a three-prong strategy. We are trying to counter them on the battlefield because of the fact that we are trying to negate this image of the caliphate which they are successfully representing. I mean, that is kind-of their center of gravity.

The second piece, as you described, is the whole cyber on-line media piece. Going back just very quickly to what Frank said, the range of options of over-the-top applications that they are able to employ. I mean, going back, I mean, what were the options that were available to al-Qaeda? Not so great. Now we are in another universe of operational activity. But, nevertheless, because they are operating in public space they have vulnerabilities there. We should move very aggressively to counter that.

Finally, the third area is this ideological space that we talked about in terms of finding those voices, those credible voices that can contest the ideological message. We need to work defense all three of those.

Mr. RATCLIFFE. Thank you, gentlemen.

I yield back. I appreciate it, Mr. Chairman.

Chairman MCCAUL. Thank you.

Mrs. Torres is recognized.

Mrs. TORRES. Thank you, Mr. Chairman.

Mr. Steinbach, I am looking forward to reading that Brooklyn Institute study on terrorism and social media. I took a sneak peak at it while we were in the session. I understand that, as of October of last year, there were 42,000 identified Twitter accounts if the report is correct, and thousands have been disabled. In some ways, I kind-of think that, you know, it is good to be able to view what is being said and what is being planned is one way we can try to prepare and prevent.

Mr. Taylor, there has been a lot of talk about community outreach programs. There has been a lot of talk about community awareness, community policing. This is nothing new. We have known that there have been a lot of issues in the past that need to be addressed from a neighborhood level. But somehow we have not been able to translate that want to do neighborhood community awareness to actually doing it.

We have seen a lot of tensions arise between our local law enforcement groups and our community groups. This is nothing recent. This has been on-going. So what have we changed? What does community policing look like in my neighborhood versus, you know, the northern part of California?

Mr. TAYLOR. Ma'am, your question is a good question. I think community policing is community policing. I don't think—it is about relationships with the communities that we serve. It hasn't changed in 20 years that I have been involved in community policing. It is the outreach that happens with people who are from the community so that you build partnerships. That is what community policing is all about.

I daresay it happens in diverse communities. It happens in majority communities. But it has to happen the same way. You have to build a relationship.

Mrs. TORRES. You need to have trust.

Mr. TAYLOR. And the trust.

Part of—Secretary Johnson has spoken eloquently about this—when he goes out to do these community engagements, he is met with skepticism. He receives complaints about profiling and other sorts of concerns the community has. But you have to have that discussion, too, to build the trust, that we are talking about things that the community needs to know that the community can do to protect themselves.

Mrs. TORRES. Thank you.

Mr. Steinbach, I know that—well, I want you to know that I represent the Ontario airport, which is, to our demise, it is controlled and managed by LAX. I would like to hear more about the FBI's Joint Terrorism Task Force in Los Angeles and how they are working with my local police department in Ontario to ensure that training is happening not only for those officers at LAX or LAPD, but it is also happening for those officers who would be the first responders should an incident happen.

Mr. STEINBACH. The LA FBI's Joint Terrorism Task Force is a very large task force. It does not just include LAX, it includes all the major airports, Orange County, Ontario. I would suggest that you make an appointment to go out and tour that. I am sure the office out there—Dave Bowdich runs that office—he would be happy to provide a tour and give you first-hand an understanding of just how robust that task force is. I was just out there a couple weeks ago discussing with him and meeting some of the folks on his task force. But I would encourage you to go out there and see first-hand.

Mrs. TORRES. Right. I would like to continue this discussion with you off the record here.

Mr. STEINBACH. Sure.

Mrs. TORRES. To bring to your attention, my staff recently went on a tour, and I was saddened to have discovered that while training is happening among other agencies, Ontario Police Department has not been invited to participate in many of that—or much of that.

Mr. STEINBACH. So I would be happy to have that conversation with you, and I also would be happy to bring those concerns to Mr. Bowdich's attention.

Mrs. TORRES. Thank you.

Mr. TAYLOR. Ma'am, if I might as well, in our community outreach role in DHS, we certainly are working very hard with police agencies throughout California. So if there is a deficit of training and there is something that DHS might be able to help in Ontario, we are more than happy to have that discussion and ensure that the training that is available in counterterrorism is available to Ontario.

Mrs. TORRES. Thank you.

Chairman MCCAUL. Mr. Katko is recognized.

Mr. KATKO. Thank you, Mr. Chairman.

I want to thank each one of you for being here today, and I have heard from some of you in the past, and I am constantly amazed at your depth of knowledge but also your dedication to your mission. I echo the sentiments of my colleagues, and I very much appreciate what you are doing to keep our country safe.

Mr. Steinbach, I want to talk to you just for a minute about the CALEA-type comments that were being made, and I just want to make sure that we are clear. I was a Federal prosecutor for 20 years and routinely engaged in all types of sophisticated wiretap surveillances and other electronic surveillances. Our investigations benefited greatly as the cellular telephone industry developed. There were many technologies that were introduced to the market that we could not at first monitor.

I think just so I am—I want to make sure we are clear what you are talking about. For those internet sites and those places on the—out there that are dark, if you will, you are simply talking about being able to have access to them. So not to monitor them without a court order, but to, obviously, to use court orders if there is probable cause to then monitor those sites. Is that what you are talking about?

Mr. STEINBACH. Absolutely correct, sir.

Mr. KATKO. Okay. So this isn't talking about just, you know, forcing them to go public so that we can monitor everything that is going on. You are talking about if you get probable cause we go forward.

Mr. STEINBACH. Going to the court with a court order, criminal courts or the FISC.

Mr. KATKO. Okay. Very good.

Mr. Taylor, you mentioned about CVE probably being our best defense against the violent extremism and the reaching out to the people that—and programs to be our best defense. I couldn't agree with you more because I was with the Chairman and others when we went overseas to talk to our foreign partners and to see first-hand the issues with the Foreign Fighter Task Force, and there are security gaps overseas that we can't control. It leads me to conclude that our best chance of stopping these instances from happening in the United States—unfortunately, it is going to be on our soil. It is not going to be overseas, at least not yet.

So, with that being said, if you could just expound for a minute, what would you envision, briefly, as to what would be the best way to build this program? I know we have got some pilot programs Nation-wide, but what would be the best way to build this program?

Mr. TAYLOR. You mean here in terms of community engagement here——

Mr. KATKO. Yes.

Mr. TAYLOR [continuing]. In our own country?

I think this is all a part of a broad set of strategies. Community engagement in this country is one part of that. I think we learned a lot of lessons from the pilot studies we have had in Los Angeles, Denver, Boston, and Minneapolis.

Mr. KATKO. Minneapolis, yes. Yep.

Mr. TAYLOR. Now the challenge is to propagate those lessons learned to communities across this country, which we are continuing to do. We believe that the first line of defense from radicalization is the family and the community and build from there. The propagation of these—this training, this engagement, we believe will help us achieve a better outcome in terms of what we are trying to get.

Mr. KATKO. Now we have the JTTF model for the law enforcement side, but from the community outreach side, I know most U.S. attorneys' offices, from example, have LECC-type coordinators. Do you envision them playing any role in this?

Mr. TAYLOR. Absolutely. It is a shared responsibility between DHS and the FBI, NCTC, and the Justice Department, and I think it is a whole-of-Government and local Government effort, not just the Federal Government. It has to be a whole community effort.

Mr. KATKO. I want to talk to—all three of you gentlemen can answer this question. The JTTFs have been the backbone of our antiterrorism efforts, and, you know, they have been—they have done a terrific job. It seems to me lately that they are under more and more stress with all the additional things that they have to look into on a regular basis. It seems that there may be more of a reliance on getting State and local law enforcement involved with the JTTFs. Is it a concern going forward, are there staffing concerns with the JTTFs going forward, and is there a concern that there are not enough Federal agents involved going forward?

Mr. STEINBACH. I would be happy to answer that question.

Mr. KATKO. It is FBI. You are going to say yes because you want more money. Right?

Mr. STEINBACH. Oh, I will say, as the head of the Counterterrorism Division of the FBI, the media reports last week were completely wrong. So the JTTF is fully staffed. The JTTF as its backbone, as you said, relies on a robust partnership with State, local, Federal, Tribal agencies. Those resources are there. They have not waned, and we certainly are not struggling to keep pace. It is a challenge. We have to prioritize our targets, but we have a very robust structure in place that relies heavily on the 17,000 State and local agencies around the country.

Mr. TAYLOR. I agree completely. I happen to have been the commander of the Air Force Office of Special Investigation when the JTTF concept was created. I supported it back in the 1990s, and I still support it today as the best law enforcement process for getting at the terrorist issues.

I think the other thing we have done—and it is not just with the JTTF—JTTF relies on fusion centers, relies on the 18,000 police organizations, first responders, and we have done a significant amount of training of those individuals, "See Something, Say Something," so that they become force multipliers for the JTTF investigators as they focus on, you know, the investigation of specific cases. So I can't speak for the resource part, but I can speak for the part that says Homeland Security, NCTC, the FBI, has invested a significant amount of training and effort to—so that people understand the threat, understand the risks, understand what to look for and report that information on a continuous basis for follow-up investigation or for intelligence to go into the IC.

Mr. KATKO. Mr. Chairman, if you indulge one brief question.

So the takeaway from this, then, is that if there is a resource issue, it is on the CVE side and—or the community outreach side, and that if something that if we can help you with, that would definitely help with the messaging.

Mr. TAYLOR. Certainly would help with the messaging and with our on-going efforts.

Mr. KATKO. Thank you all, gentlemen, very much.

Chairman MCCAUL. Thank you.

Mr. Keating is recognized.

Mr. KEATING. Thank you, Mr. Chairman.

Two incidents just this week really demonstrated to me the prevalence of what this committee hearing is about today in terms of the internet and that as a recruitment device. It hit really close to home.

One of them was the killing of Ahmad Abousamra. He—you know, he was educated. He went to school just a few miles from where I went to school and where my children went to school, and became radicalized. As you are aware, he was among—he was on the FBI's Ten Most Wanted List, and he also was the architect, one of the major architects, of what we are discussing here today, where he was fashioning the internet message in a very sophisticated way. He was killed in northern Iraq during the last week.

Then, second, in the area I used to represent in the legislature, the neighborhood in Boston, where the terrorist incident occurred. I want to congratulate you on your work, your fine work, in dealing with that where there were reports where that was linked, at least the reports out there on there in an on-going investigation, public reports, that was linked to this kind of on-going recruitment through the internet.

So I look at those things, and I understand the importance of information sharing on one end. What we concluded with the Boston Marathon bombing, the importance of both the local, State, and Federal Government working together to share that information. I want to congratulate you all on moving that forward and improving that situation.

I think it is very clear, although it is not happening this moment in terms of maybe even actionable threats, but at least incidents that have occurred, we are going to have to expand that to local government, State government, Federal Government, and international because it is just a matter of time before many of these linkages materialize in a concrete fashion.

I want to ask two questions: No. 1, given the fact that it is going to be four areas, not just three, of information sharing, we came back, several Members of the this committee, from a CODEL, and we understand the difficulties in—particularly in the Europe area with our allies where they are not moving forward with passenger name records, which we take for granted here, when anyone makes a reservation. Having border security even on the exterior of the European Union borders and how that is not moving the way it should as quickly as it should, and even the technical support that we offer as a country to some of these countries as to how to deal with it not being utilized.

So I want to ask on a couple of fronts. No. 1, I still think we can work together with countries, even if the European Union isn't moving. I want you to comment on how we are dealing with that information sharing, local, State, Federal, and with those individual countries because we also found that some countries are more receptive and moving faster than others in terms of information sharing that will make us all safer, not just here and not just when Americans travel abroad in Europe, but here at home too.

The other thing is the idea that, you know, we are doing a good job swatting mosquitoes here at home when it comes to the internet, but we are not drying up the swamp as much as we can. Can you comment on what we are doing for counter-messaging, not just enforcement or trying to find out what is going on, but in counter-messaging through the internet to try and have competing messages and what you think more could be done? So those are the two questions, and anyone that wants to address those.

Mr. MULLIGAN. So I will jump in on the first piece with regard to—and, again, my colleagues are more conversant on pushing the information to the locals. But from a National perspective, we are very consciously trying to push the intelligence and the knowledge that has been gleaned from our assessments down to the locals so that they are more fully informed. That is definitely—and we need to do more and we have to keep pushing that.

On the international piece that you described, it does become at times very unwieldy when you make it a multi-lateral issue. So we have established a number of very close bi-lateral relationships in terms of information sharing that has been very, very positive.

But the challenge is, if you really are going to try and address these challenges in a time-efficient way, you need to ensure that a broader range is—that you have the equipment that you can be passing information effectively. So that is a longer-term objective in that regard.

In terms of the overall counter-messaging, the Government—our Government, our Federal Government, has an interagency process involved in which we are all moving to do counter-messaging, that counter-messaging works at the speed of Government. It is—well, as you understand, it has constraints in that I think the real secret is going to be to broaden that overall counter-messaging and include those folks outside of the Government so that they can participate in that process.

Mr. TAYLOR. I would make two comments, sir.

First, this committee has been very clear to me in my role as the under secretary for intelligence and analysis that the core customer for the intelligence that we do is State and locals. We have worked very hard for the last year to try to transform how we approach the dissemination of data and information to our State and local partners with our IC colleagues, with the FBI, and with others, and NCTC, but specifically focusing on getting relevant information out quickly to our State and local partners. I don't know how many Joint Intelligence Bulletins we have done this year, but I think it is a record over last year. So that is our commitment, to move this information and get it into the hands of our first responders at the State, local, Federal, Tribal, and private sector.

When we talk about our foreign partners, you mentioned the European Union. The European Union is, in some cases, reluctant to use PNR across to all the European Union. We do have individual dialogues with members of the European Union where certain countries are moving forward to do that within their own country. I think I was just on the—in New York at the United Nations with Secretary Johnson. We talked about U.N. Security Council Resolution 1267. I think there is more pressure on those communities to do that, and we will continue to press to get those kinds of laws passed in those countries for that kind of information.

I would also emphasize that all of the Visa Waiver countries—and that is most of the European Union—have independent bilateral agreements with us on information sharing. Now, it may be through the intelligence service, it may be through the FBI or law enforcement. Those are very robust agreements that we are continuing to press for the exchange of that kind of information. So it is not a perfect scene yet, but the information exchange both within our country, to our State and local partners, and also with our foreign partners continues to improve on a daily basis.

Chairman McCAUL. Mr. Loudermilk is recognized.

Mr. LOUDERMILK. Thank you, Mr. Chairman.

Thank you all for being here. Of all the hearings that we have had, in my opinion, this has been one of the most productive and informative that I have sat in on.

One of the things that we are going to be doing in my office in the coming weeks is visiting with local law enforcement, our fusion centers within the district because what I am seeing with this lone-wolf attacks, the calls for attackers that are already in the United States, there is going to be a reliance on local law enforcement. With the recent attacks, it is a reminder to me, and I think to all of us, that these attacks are not against us as individuals, they are not against us as citizens. They are attacks by those who are threatened or diametrically opposed to what we are as a people and what we have, which is freedom. You know, our freedom of thought, freedom of ideas, freedom of religion and, in the case of Garland, Texas, was the freedom of speech. That was really what was being attacked.

With that in mind, the American Freedom Defense Initiative and their contest seems to be—as some have said—incited these attacks. Understanding and knowing what happened with *Charlie Hebdo* in Paris, which I was there just a few weeks ago in Paris with this codel, it would lead us to believe that this is a potential target. The first question, how far in advance of the event did our IC or counterterrorism know that this event was happening? How did we find that out? Was there a coordination with them, or did this come from local law enforcement?

Mr. STEINBACH. We knew about it several weeks in advance. More specifically, I will say, in this event, in the event in Phoenix last Friday, and in every event like this, we do go to those organizers and individuals and lay out the threats and the potential. We, of course, don't try to talk them out of it, but we explain to them: Hey. If you do X, this may happen. So we knew several weeks in advance.

Mr. LOUDERMILK. Okay. So you know that these are coming. How much interface do you have with the local law enforcement going into these?

Mr. STEINBACH. It is multi-faceted. So, you know, we put out a joint intelligence bulletin which lays out, in this case in Garland, a week in advance, kind-of laid out the events and the threat to the events. In this particular case and in many events like it, we push out a communication tool called a collection emphasis message. That collection emphasis message asks agencies, Federal,

State, and local, to collect intelligence on the event and the threats. We put out tactical reports. We have, in many cases, depending on the size of the event, we have preparatory meetings with State and local, identifying who is going to have lead for crowd control, emergency response, tactical resources. It is a multi-layered approach we take with every special event.

Mr. LOUDERMILK. Now Miss Rice asked one of the questions I was getting at which was we have 15 years of tracking terrorism, terrorists, and their activities, their threats through all the chatter. So we have kind-of got to where we can filter through what is just chatter and what is a valid threat.

How responsive are local law enforcement to the threats that we are laying out? You know, do they tend to take them seriously?

Mr. STEINBACH. Yes. We spend a lot of time, DHS, NCTC, and the FBI, pushing that message at the local level through the field offices as well as at the executive level.

Just 2 weeks ago, we had a video teleconference that was led by the director of the FBI and the director of Homeland Security, where we lay out, again, the threat, the current threat. We do that periodically. So there are multiple levels of engagement. Today I am going to be taking to major city chiefs on this same topic.

Mr. TAYLOR. I would add, sir, that we have created a network in our fusion centers with our JTTFs across this country. Whenever an event occurs, there is someone up on the net saying: What is the impact on my community? That is done over the Homeland Security intelligence network, or it is done over the law enforcement network of the FBI. Our local law enforcement partners understand their primary responsibility to protect their communities. They understand these risks threaten their communities. They are hungry for information to help them prepare. That is what we try to design is a system that gets that information out to them. Once they get it, as they did in Garland, they take the appropriate action.

Mr. LOUDERMILK. Now, and if some of this—these questions are more of a Classified nature, we can respond to those later because I understand and appreciate being in the intelligence community in the past.

But of the communications that we know that happen between the attackers and other bad players, how much of that did we know before the attack versus as forensic information, and how much of that played into the warning that we sent to the local?

Mr. STEINBACH. I would be happy to answer that, but not in this setting.

Mr. LOUDERMILK. Okay. I appreciate that.

The last one is the reverse flow. Do we have good channels of communications for intelligence gathering from local law enforcement, who are the boots on the ground in the community, that—because, you know, this was a National event per se because it was an organization out of New York, but you may have a local event that could be a high-threat target. Do we have a flow of information up from the locals?

Mr. TAYLOR. Sir, it is a great question. Again, under the direction from this committee, we have worked to expand the amount of local intelligence that is gathered and reported into the IC that is relevant to the IC, not only working with the FBI but working independently with our fusion centers in the field. We have created a new process, what we call field activity reporting, where fusion centers working with DHS and the FBI will do reports from a field—State-level perspective on threats and risks in the community.

So I think we have created that opportunity for the local, State and local partners to report up, for us to report down, and for all of us to share information on a continuous basis.

Mr. LOUDERMILK. Are they actively reporting up?

Mr. TAYLOR. Absolutely, sir.

Mr. STEINBACH. Let me highlight that a little bit more, sir.

So, I mean, the reason we are pushing information out is to make use of the 400,000 State, local, and Tribal law enforcement officers around the country. They are our first response. They are the ones doing the car stop. They are the ones going to the house as the first responders. They are seeing it well before any of us here see it. It is incumbent we have the guardian process that allows for reporting, the e-guardian process that allows for reporting of information quickly into the fusion center and the JTTF model to act on that. So that is the crux, and that is really at the foundation of this process.

Mr. LOUDERMILK. All right. Thank you very much.

Mr. Chairman.

Chairman MCCAUL. Ms. McSally is recognized.

Ms. MCSALLY. Thank you, Mr. Chairman.

Thank you, gentlemen for your testimony today. I appreciate, as part of our Task Force on Combating Terrorism and Foreign Fighter Flow, we have had some other conversations in Classified settings. So I appreciate all the work that you are doing.

Question I have today is about—first one is about the recruitment of women and girls from our country. It seems that jihadi women in Syria are actively recruiting—or not just women, recruiting Western girls. I, you know, can't imagine what the draw would be, except of course they are being lied to like most of the recruits. But here we have American girls that are being recruited to potentially flow over there for a life of rape and slavery. So specifically of about—I think you said there is 200 that we know of Americans that have flowed over to the region, how many of them are women and girls, and are there specific targeting efforts that we are doing community-wide or others in order to address specifically what is going on with targeting of women and girls?

Mr. STEINBACH. So I won't get into specific numbers, but, you know, when you look 5, 6 years ago, the number of female recruits was almost nil. So right now it is 10 percent I think is probably a good ballpark. So it is a minority, but the fact that it went from zero to where it is at now is a significant uptick for us. So, yes, we look at the reasons why individuals are recruited, the specifics. Young adult males, young adult females, what is drawing them?

That is part of our process to understand it, what the motivation is for radicalization. We find a wide variety. It is not just the classic—you see on TV—jihadi bride. There are other reasons that are motivating these young women to take a chance and go overseas.

Ms. MCSALLY. So and as part of the countering of it and engaging with communities actually—do we have messages of, ''No, you are going to be in slavery and repeatedly raped when you get over there,'' and actually countering that in, you know, the graphic reality of what they are going to get recruited into to include potentially testimonies of individuals that have experienced this. I mean, the way you counter a message is with a stronger message.

Mr. STEINBACH. Absolutely.

Ms. MCSALLY. So we are doing some of that——

Mr. STEINBACH. Absolutely.

Ms. MCSALLY [continuing]. At the local level as well?

Mr. STEINBACH. Yes. Through the JTTFs or the fusion centers. As part of the CVE narrative, we are reaching out, you know, pushing the message out to the communities, to the schools, having conversations about the dangers of being on-line, not just on-line because of pedophiles and because of cyber criminals but on-line for fear of recruitment and enticement.

Ms. MCSALLY. Right. Okay. Great. Thanks.

My next question is about the use of social media for fundraising and wonder if you could comment on how ISIS is using social media in order to raise funds through crowd-sourcing and other, you know, attempts to raise funds using social media, and are you working with the Department of Treasury, specific offices of asset forfeiture, FinCEN and OFAC? Specifically, how successful have they been and how are we countering that fundraising?

Mr. MULLIGAN. I would characterize it for you as it is a very arduous process to rebuild—or build our understanding of the financial processes that ISIS and ISIL is employing currently. I would also point out, as you probably are very well aware, that they are—in their expansion of the caliphate, they are literally taking possession of a number of resources and then exploiting that. So, to a large extent, they have been able to draw on a lot of those resources for a lot of their financing and funding. But, nevertheless, it is a long—and because of the fact that they are an extended organization, they have to manage that financial infrastructure. That is an intelligence effort that is underway. We are working very aggressively with the Treasury Department and other stakeholders.

Ms. MCSALLY. So their on-line fundraising is miniscule compared to how their—I mean, I know black market and all the stuff they are doing in the regions that they have and the ransoms and all the things that they have done that we are focusing on, but specifically the on-line fundraising.

Mr. MULLIGAN. I would qualify it by saying I don't think that we are seeing the same degree of on-line fundraising that we probably have seen in the past by other entities.

Mr. STEINBACH. I would concur with that.

Ms. MCSALLY. Yeah. Okay. Great.

My last question really quickly is, we know ISIS has been trying to motivate people to attack military bases or attack military members. Obviously, you know, I was in the military, those are some of our most secure areas. There is, you know, certainly softer targets that they could go after, but if they were to recruit somebody who has access to a base, Major Hasan as an example, you know, we could have a major impact from an insider threat.

Have you seen ISIS attempting to recruit military members or those who have access to bases? Are you working with the Department of Defense in order to counter that threat?

Mr. TAYLOR. Well, as the Chairman mentioned in his opening remarks, the Department of Defense takes this threat very seriously. They work very closely with the FBI, the IC, and DHS around how those risks are—might manifest themselves within the country.

Your point earlier, it is a pretty secure place, but they have even identified people by addresses, and we work with the military on strategies for those individuals to protect themselves at this point.

Ms. MCSALLY. Okay.

Any other comments?

Mr. MULLIGAN. Wanted to just offer the fact that it is very reasonable to expect a very aggressive effort by ISIS to be trying to derive military targets because part of their overall narrative is the fact they want to draw linkages. They want to make those correlations. So we have to be particularly vigilant with regard to military members.

Ms. MCSALLY. Great. Thank you.

My time is expired. Thank you, Mr. Chairman.

Chairman MCCAUL. Let me thank the witnesses for your testimony and your service to our country.

The Members may have additional questions in writing, and pursuant to committee rule 7(C), the hearing will be open—record open for 10 days. Without objection, the committee stands adjourned.

[Whereupon, at 12:29 p.m., the committee was adjourned.]